THE COMPLETE BOOK OF
WILD SWIMMING IN IRELAND

Maureen McCoy is a swimming coach and an award-winning open-water swimmer. As a coach she has been involved with training and mentoring the new wave of swim teachers and coaches. She was Irish 17km champion and in 2009 achieved her childhood dream of swimming the English Channel.

Having swum in the sea, loughs and rock pools with her brothers since she was a small child, she also competed in swim events in Ireland, the UK and Alaska. She no longer competes but still enjoys outdoor swimming throughout the year and always keeps a swimsuit in her car – just in case.

Paul McCambridge has been a multi-award-winning photojournalist and features photographer for over 35 years. His work has been exhibited nationally and published internationally. Paul received the Simon Cumbers Media Fund in 2012 and 2015 for his photojournalism on human trafficking in the Bay of Bengal.

Representing Ulster as a swimmer in his youth, Paul kept his hand in as a voluntary coach and kept swimming for fitness. In the open water, he has medalled in several races and completed a North Channel relay in 2011. He is now expanding his skills to film-making and has recently produced the film *Man of Arran*.

Pedlar's Lake, Dingle Peninsula

THE COMPLETE BOOK OF
WILD SWIMMING
IN IRELAND

MAUREEN McCOY
& PAUL McCAMBRIDGE

GILL BOOKS

Gill Books
Hume Avenue
Park West
Dublin 12
www.gillbooks.ie

Gill Books is an imprint of M.H. Gill and Co.

978 18045 8068 4

Designed by grahamthew.com
Edited by Paula Elmore
Proofread by Jane Rogers
Printed and bound by L.E.G.O. SpA, Italy
This book is typeset in 9.5pt Elena Basic

The paper used in this book comes from the wood pulp of
sustainably managed forests.

A CIP catalogue record for this book is available from the
British Library.

**DISCLAIMER: Swimming is a risk sport. *The Complete
Book of Wild Swimming in Ireland* is not a guide to
swimming safety. Neither the authors nor the publisher
accept any responsibility for damage, injury or loss of
any kind, to property or persons, that occurs directly
or indirectly from the use of this book or from any
water-based activity.**

5 4 3 2 1

CONTENTS

LEINSTER

MUNSTER

CONNACHT

INTRODUCTION

Our first book, *Wild Swimming in Ireland: Discover 50 Places to Swim in Rivers, Lakes & The Sea*, was a labour of love. What could be better for swimmers than to explore the entire country with a tent and a map with the sole purpose of hunting out swimming spots?

Lockdown and the surge of people getting outside and rediscovering swimming meant that now was time to renew our efforts.

This book contains 49 of the original 50 sites and adds much more. We've chosen places we really like; some are dips, some have caves or arches and some are suitable for long-distance swims.

Let us take you on a swimming adventure through Ireland, exploring the coast, lakes and rivers searching for hidden gems and forgotten treasures. Swim under the Carrick-a-Rede rope bridge on the rugged Ulster coast where the chilly North Sea challenges swimmers; jump into mountain loughs with the most amazing scenery; travel along the Wild Atlantic Way, Europe's longest designated coastal route, to explore the beautiful hidden beaches and coves; visit Galway, famed for vibrant music sessions that go on all night and plunge from the dual-aspect high-diving boards or do a spot of beachcombing at the multicoloured Coral Beach.

City swimming in Dublin is popular. Find the best places to go, from the Forty Foot to the Vico. Journey to the beaches of the sunny south-east, then head south-west to Waterford's rugged Copper Coast and the dramatic peninsulas of Kerry. Finally, head north to Donegal and its myriad of beaches and coves.

In this book, you will find a wonderful guide to the waters in and around Ireland and excellent tips on making the exploration a safe and enjoyable experience for all. With advice on equipment, swimming skills and selecting swim challenges that suit you, we hope this book inspires you to keep swimming and keep exploring.

Safe swimming

If you can swim, you can swim outdoors. Wild swimming is only dangerous if swimmers take unnecessary risks. Common sense and a little preparation can make the experience safe and enjoyable for all.

Outdoor swimming has grown fast in popularity, folks are hitting the water year round, but this is not a controlled environment; conditions change all the time. Wind, tides, temperatures, river flow: you will never have the same swim twice. This is what makes it so exciting and why we keep coming back for more.

Never swim alone

The number one rule of swimming: always swim with a buddy. Keep an eye on each other, ensuring that neither is getting cold or tired. Leave the water together.

Swim parallel to the shore

Swimming straight out, particularly in the sea, can lead to mishaps. Imagine if the tide is also moving out; you then turn and realise you have been aided by the outgoing tide and are in fact a lot farther from shore than you thought. You are now battling the tide to return.

Swimming parallel to the shore means you can easily get back to dry land.

Get out while you still want more

As we become tired or cold it becomes more difficult for us to swim (see 'Swim failure' below). By choosing wisely when to leave the water, we will come out thinking 'I can't wait for my next swim!' rather than 'I never want to go through that again!'

Watch the weather

Do not try to swim in rough conditions: no matter how strong you think you are, the water is always more powerful. It is very difficult to breathe or navigate in choppy water. In fog, you will lose your bearings and will not be visible to others.

Know your limits

Be aware of your own swimming ability, how well you can function in the cold, your ability to read the conditions and your knowledge of currents and tides. If you are less confident, stay within your depth and close to an exit point.

Be visible

Wear a bright swimming cap and a tow-float to make yourself visible to any craft in the area.

Floating and treading water

All swimmers should be able to float and tread water with complete ease. Practise both these skills. Floating can get you out of a tricky situation: if you are tired, cold or heading into swim failure, lean onto your back, spread arms and legs and focus on your breath. When treading water, again stay relaxed, arms wide and making a sculling action, legs wide and either a slow breaststroke action or a slow-motion running action – the wider you make your body the easier it is to keep your head up.

Never dive into unfamiliar water

Check the depth and for any obstacles. Cold-water shock can debilitate the strongest of swimmers (even causing loss of consciousness). Walk in slowly, acclimatise and settle your breathing.

RIGHT Barley Harbour, County Longford

Seek advice

Ask about conditions, water quality, hazards or currents. Tide tables are readily available to download to your phone. Keep an eye on the weather: wind can play a major role in determining the strength and chop of waves.

Food and drink

Never swim within two hours of a meal and NEVER after ANY alcohol.

Cold-water shock

Recent findings state that around 60 per cent of drownings in Britain and Ireland are due to cold shock response; the immediate physical response we have to sudden cold causes involuntary inhalation. In waters around 15°C, it is extremely difficult for even strong swimmers to hold their breath when suddenly immersed. It takes an inhalation of only 1.5 litres of water to drown an adult.

The solution? DO NOT jump straight in. Get in slowly, wet your arms and face, lower yourself in gently, swim head up at first to acclimatise, and control your breathing. Then, once your breathing has settled, you can swim face in.

Swim failure

This can happen to any swimmer, and will happen if you stay in too long. As our body cools, our muscle strength and function are depleted and our nerves lose the ability to send messages to the muscles. Ever had that feeling that your little finger won't be controlled? This is an early sign. As we get colder, the arms lose the ability to function properly, the legs begin to drop and we have entered swim failure. Learn your own 'tells'. Is it the little finger popping out? Or perhaps your breathing becomes more laboured? As your swimming function decreases, you are at risk. Don't take that risk; leave the water. You can come back another day.

Swim failure can and does happen to channel swimmers but several elements minimise the likelihood: channel/marathon swimmers often have an extremely efficient stroke with a good body position in the water; it takes longer for their stroke to break down to the point of serious risk; they have trained for distance and cold tolerance; and they are constantly monitored by a support team who will note any stroke speed or strength changes; they will also have regular feed stops to help them retain energy for both swimming and generating heat.

After-drop

Body temperature drops quickly in the water and it continues to drop for around twenty minutes post-swim. Get dried quickly and put on warm clothes (layers are best) and have a hot drink after your swim.

Brackley Lough, County Cavan

River swimming

If you are intending to do an out-and-back swim, it is best to head upstream first and then return with the flow of the river helping you. It is surprising how what may seem like very little current can be extremely difficult to counter, especially when you are tired.

Waterfalls

Waterfalls are beautiful places but there can be hidden dangers: fresh water is less buoyant than sea water; the force of the water coming down from the fall can be enough to push a swimmer under; debris can gather both above and below. Check the depth and also for debris and be cautious about swimming under the fall itself. Know your own ability.

Lake swimming

Lakes tend to warm up and cool down more quickly than sea water, some getting icy in winter. They are also more susceptible to quality issues, such as blue/green algal blooms and run-off from agriculture. Heed any signs warning of poor water quality.

Please enjoy yourselves and SWIM SAFE.

ESSENTIAL KIT

A SENSE OF ADVENTURE!

All outdoor swimmers have a little rebel streak in them. Celebrate that and enjoy the exploration of new places, or old ones seen from a new perspective.

SWIM SENSE

It seems tedious to reiterate but use your noggin! If your gut feeling is that it is a bad idea, it probably is. Confidence is all very well but competence is key: know your own limitations, your swimming ability and capacity to deal with the cold. Seek advice from others, start gently, and enjoy building your confidence, skill and power in the water.

DRY CLOTHING

After a swim your body temperature will drop, so get dried and dressed quickly. Too many layers are better than too few.

DESIRABLE KIT

SWIMSUIT

Essential at popular beaches, although there are plenty of places where this is optional!

GOGGLES

Great for seeing clearly underwater and keeping your eyeballs from feeling as if they are going to freeze in winter. Goggles have a nasty habit of steaming up, though, so prepare them beforehand (rub with a smear of baby shampoo and then wipe dry, or a generous amount of spit).

CAP

Keeps hair out of the eyes, can help minimise water in the ears (when pulled down enough) and provides a layer of insulation. Caps come in a range of types, styles and, of course, colours. Go for bright neon colours that are easily seen. Silicone caps beat latex for thickness and insulation and are less likely to tear. Neoprene hoods give more insulation, but swimmers used to caps may find the chinstrap inhibiting.

CHANGING TOWEL

Keeps you decent on busy beaches and provides something of a windbreak. There are many on the market and budget is your only limitation. I still love my trusty handcrafted version, modelled on the ones Mum made for my brothers and me when we were small.

TOW FLOATS

These are NOT life-saving equipment so do not rely on them. They can be useful if you need a short rest on a long swim but remember that your temperature will drop very quickly when you are inactive in the water. Some of these floats are designed to carry a drinks bottle: useful when doing long training swims.

FLASK OF HOT BEVERAGE

Smooth, creamy and indulgent hot chocolate is a popular choice but any hot drink is a great way to warm up after a swim. Most will accompany this with a sweet snack.

Bull Island, County Dublin

HOT-WATER BOTTLE

Part of my essential winter kit, either already filled, with my socks tucked inside the cover (heavenly!) or a spare flask of hot water ready to fill it when I get out.

DRY BAG

A large dry bag for your towels and dry clothes, and a small dry bag for car keys (I personally like to double-bag my key and bring it with me – just in case – and I always keep a spare towel, fleece and jogging bottoms in the car, in case someone thinks it funny to nick my gear from the beach).

THERMAL UNDIES

Not the most flattering but they are simply great.

VERY WARM BOOTS

After the swim, especially a winter swim, pulling on a fleece-lined boot is oh so nice – you can stuff disposable hand warmers into your socks, too.

OPTIONAL EXTRAS

WETSUIT

Wetsuits provide a great deal of insulation and some buoyancy. Thanks to the rising popularity of triathlon and open-water swimming, there is now a good range of affordable wetsuits. Try before you buy. If you are going to use it mostly for swimming, get a suit specifically designed for triathlons. The heavy surfing-type wetsuits may keep you warm but do not have the flexibility around the arms and shoulders to allow for the freedom of movement swimmers need. Many swimmers find the necklines tight on wetsuits so get used to the suit before you head out for your epic swim. If you are already a wetsuit swimmer, next time you are out, take a few minutes at the end of your swim to cast aside the suit and try a quick dip 'skins' – you might just love it!

Exploring the North Antrim coast

NEOPRENE GLOVES AND SHOES

Many find their fingers get cold and gloves can add a layer of insulation. I find them heavy to swim with, but others swear by them. Shoes are extremely useful if you are likely to be clambering over rocks as they provide good grip and protection. Great to keep toes a little warmer in winter, too.

MASK, SNORKEL, FINS

Great fun for exploring the underwater world. There is a surprising array of sea creatures to see in Ireland's clear waters. Fins can give you a lot of speed and, if they fit well, you can catch more waves to bodysurf.

WATERPROOF CAMERA

It is amazing how much wildlife there is to see in our waters. Beware, though, of taking those 'arty pics' half-under and half-above the water – your subject may not find the resulting image entirely flattering!

HAND WARMERS

Disposable ones are warmer but the reusable ones are a little more environmentally friendly. A hot-water bottle may do the same job. There is a wealth of other gear on the market – gloves, swim floats, lifebuoys – the choice is yours.

GLOW STICKS

For night swimming, a glow stick tucked into the goggle strap allows others to see the swimmer.

The most important piece of equipment you have is yourself – your own competence and judgement.

BEST REASONS TO SWIM OUTDOORS

'Going swimming' now means a day trip to the beach or lake or mountains with a warm-up drink and scone after, or, better still, the pub where you can cosy up to the fire while sipping Guinness.

BOOSTS THE IMMUNE SYSTEM

This is not yet backed up by medical evidence, but any year-round swimmer will tell you that when they swim through the winter, they simply don't get a cold.

FEEL-GOOD FACTOR

Undoubtedly the best reason for doing it is that it's fun! Studies have shown that it can increase our 'happy hormones': dopamine, serotonin, endorphins and oxytocin.

STRESS RELIEVER

In addition to the effects of the above hormone release, the process of focusing purely on one thing – our swimming or our breathing – can be great for stress relief. Many of us find swimming a meditative activity.

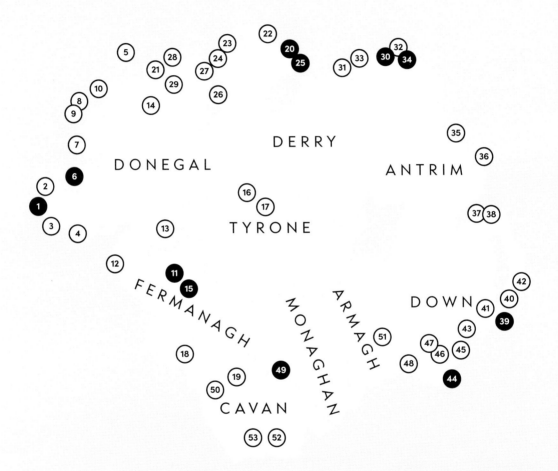

ULSTER

BLESSED WITH SOME OF THE best beaches in Ireland, Donegal is a wild and varied landscape; travelling from the far west we take a jaunt out to Tory Island and Árainn Mhór, with probably the nicest ferry ride in the country! Skirt along the north coast visiting *Game of Thrones* locations all the way down to Lecale and the Mourne Mountains. Inland, we visit the lakes of Fermanagh and Cavan for a taste of the best of freshwater swimming.

❶ SILVER STRAND

COUNTY DONEGAL

On the far western shores of Donegal not far from the great cliffs of Slieve League sits the pretty curve of Silver Strand at Malin Beg, 400m of golden sand beside a small harbour favoured by divers.

Venture west from Donegal town, along the N59, through the towns of Inver and Killybegs, which both have popular beaches, towards the impressive Slieve League, which is among the highest of the sea cliffs in Ireland and, at over 600m, rivals the Cliffs of Moher. To the south the rock has been carved by the sea and weather to form a knife-like edge rising to the summit. The road winds up to a viewpoint close to the top, overlooking majestic Donegal Bay. Far below, the Giant's Desk and Giant's Chair are two rock formations easily identifiable in the cove.

Six kilometres from Glencolumbkille is the pretty Silver Strand at Malin Beg. It is a steep climb down the steps from the car park to the enticing white sands of the horseshoe-shaped bay but worth every bit of effort. At approximately 400m long and with gently shelving waters, this beach provides excellent swimming and, set as it is down such a flight of steps, the strand is never crowded. Nestled beneath grassy headlands, it is as close to a perfect beach as you may find. Count the steps going down and on the way back up, and see if you can get the same number!

The nearby harbour at Malin Beg is rich in sea life, making it popular with divers and snorkellers. The harbour is set in a neat natural cove, making it extremely well sheltered.

Swim from the harbour steps, turning right towards the small sea stack approximately 90m out and look along the shore on your right; just beyond the cottage there is an archway leading to a tiny gravel beach. It is always exciting to explore the darkness of a cave or arch. The tiny beach itself is sunk down behind the road and looks a little like a grotto.

⑤

DONEGAL

RIGHT Silver Strand

AT A GLANCE

① SILVER STRAND

The magnificent curved beach of Silver Strand close to the sheer cliffs of Slieve League. Be prepared for the steep climb back up the steps to the car park. Snorkel at Malin Beg Harbour where there is abundant sea life, or duck through the arch to the right of the harbour to a minute gravel beach.

BY CAR: 65 minutes from Donegal town. Take N56 west along the shore of Donegal Bay, then R263 through Killybegs. Carry on along R263 to Glencolumbkille with its two beaches, the smaller of which is more private. **For Silver Strand**, continue on R263 from Glencolumbkille for 6km to the end of the road and the clifftop car park. **For Malin Beg Harbour**, turn right just after Malinbeg Hostel. This road leads down to the harbour.

SCENIC WALK • STEEP STEPS TO BEACH • HARBOUR AND COVE TO SWIM OR SNORKEL • SEA ARCH TO TINY SHALE BEACH • HOSTEL AND CAFÉ NEARBY • FAMILY FRIENDLY

GRID REF: G 50333 79655
GOOGLE MAPS REF:
54.66450, -8.77755

② GLENCOLUMBKILLE BEACH

Best known for the Oideas Gael, the Irish-language school set up in 1984, the village draws students of all ages from all over the world. Glencolumbkille also has two pretty beaches with easy access from the village. The first is the larger and shelves gently into the bracing Atlantic. **Not suitable for children** as it has a large sand bank which can create eddy currents. The second beach is to the right and overlooked by a pretty cottage. A steep, narrow track leads down to the strand which is away from the sand bank and shelves a little more steeply. At low water you can walk between the two beaches.

Check out the Folk Village to see how people lived and worked in the 18th to 20th centuries or walk one of three loop walks: 5km, 8km and 13km.

BY CAR: 55 minutes from Donegal town. Take N56 west through Inver, onto R263 to Killybegs. Continue 24km to the village.

CURRENTS • TWO BEACHES • SUITABLE FOR STRONG SWIMMERS ONLY

GRID REF: G 52358 85029
GOOGLE MAPS REF:
54.70905, -8.74009

③ PORTACOWLEY BEACH

Tucked in beside the mouth of the River Glen, this small patch of sand is a gem of a beach. Teelin Pier, where you can take a Slieve League boat tour, is visible across the sheltered bay. The hills behind rise up steeply and in the distance is the great hulk of Slieve League itself. Safe for children, this spot is used in the summer for lessons and it's easy to see the appeal. At high water there may be little beach so be sure to keep your gear high up on the bank if you take a longer swim!

BY CAR: 47 minutes from Donegal town. Take N56 west for 23.5km, then R263 to Killybegs. Continue 10km, then turn left through Kilcar. After 3.5km, turn sharp left, signed Trá; 1km along this road brings you to the little beach. Park on the roadside and walk the track down to the beach. Limited roadside parking.

SECLUDED • FAMILY FRIENDLY

GRID REF: G 59509 75916
GOOGLE MAPS REF:
54.63019, -8.62835

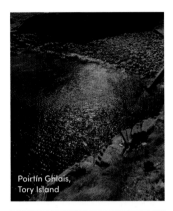

Poirtín Ghlais,
Tory Island

Trabane, St John's Point Beach

Portacowley Beach

④ TRABANE, ST JOHN'S POINT BEACH

Near the end of the narrow peninsula that juts out between McSwyne's Bay and Donegal Bay is the east-facing Trabane. A gently shelving sandy bay, it's perfect for all levels of swimmer: children can play in the shallows while stronger swimmers do laps. At 375m across, it makes for a lovely training ground. The narrow road bringing you here has superb views across McSwyne's Bay and when you reach the beach, you are treated to views back towards the large expanse of Rossnowlagh. The 1.5km walk out to the lighthouse rewards you with 360-degree views, taking in east and west Donegal and south to Sligo.

BY CAR: 30 minutes from Donegal town. Take N56 west 18km. Turn left onto L1435/St John's Point. Continue for 8km to the beach. Limited parking.

FAMILY FRIENDLY • BEAUTIFUL VIEWS • LOWLAND WALK TO LIGHTHOUSE

GRID REF: G 71646 70058
GOOGLE MAPS REF: 54.57919, -8.43994

⑤ POIRTÍN GHLAIS, TORY ISLAND

This northern shore of Tory Island has high cliffs, taking all the battery of the sea, the rocks flayed with lines as though the sea and wind have whipped them repeatedly, creating scars. Derek Hill, portrait and landscape painter, returned here over many years, working in a tiny hut. Close by, a small bench looks towards a curved metal barrier, a viewpoint to the inlet below. A steep, narrow stone staircase leads down to the water. On a calm day, perfection!

Tory Island lies 13km as the crow flies from Magheroarty pier. The ferry runs regularly.

BY CAR: 25 minutes from Dunfanaghy, take N56 west 16.5km. Turn right onto R257; after 1.5km, turn right to stay on R257 for 2km, then right down to the pier and ferry (the 45-minute boat trip runs three times daily). Once on the island, walk the track north from the town to Poirtín Ghlais, the small harbour below Derek Hill's Hut, approx. 1km away. Only suitable in calm conditions. Pick up a map of the island at the ferry office.

DIVING • SUITABLE FOR STRONG SWIMMERS ONLY

GRID REF: B 84924 47056
GOOGLE MAPS REF: 55.27064, -8.23785

⑥ TRAMORE

COUNTY DONEGAL

When the citizens and businesspeople of Ardara found they had been bypassed by the Wild Atlantic Way, their roads being considered too narrow for the large tourist coaches, in true entrepreneurial style they set up their own scenic route to entice smaller vehicles and cyclists. Follow the Wild Atlantic Bay signs; the icon of a crossed-out coach showing the roads will be narrow, winding and tricky. However, there is a fitting prize for the effort.

North of Ardara, take a left turn where the Wild Atlantic Bay sign guides you and pass through mature vegetation into rugged and craggy low hills. Another left turn signed to Tramore Beach and Caravan Park brings you first to Sheskinmore Nature Reserve. The reserve gate is on the roadside. There is car parking space at a lay-by and a basic map of the reserve. One of the most important reserves in Ireland, Sheskinmore covers around a thousand acres of marsh and sand dunes. Many different species of butterfly are to be found here, alongside many rare orchids. Wildlife is plentiful, including badgers, foxes and otters and, in the sky, peregrine falcons and merlin.

A 3km walk through the dunes leads to the wide expanse of the almost deserted Ballinreavy Strand. To walk from here along to Tramore Strand, veer right and follow the shoreline; alternatively, return to your car and follow the road down to a small parking area by the entrance to the caravan park. Walk to the beach on the sandy track along which tiny mushrooms grow at the base of the sand grasses, looking like a curious miniature forest.

The beach of stunning fine white sand shelves very gradually. This large beach never gets crowded, the campsite is small and tucked behind the dunes and the area has a wild and exposed feel. There may be the occasional solitary walker and, near the site, children enjoying the surf. At the far end of the beach, you can have the dunes and sea all to yourself.

DONEGAL

ABOVE AND LEFT Flora at Tramore, County Donegal

AT A GLANCE

⑥ TRAMORE

Tramore is a lovely white sand beach with dunes behind. Walk through the nature reserve where you may see falcons hunting.

BY CAR: 1 hour 25 minutes from Donegal town. Take N56 west, then north to Ardara. Continue north of Ardara on R261 towards Portnoo. After 6km, take a left towards Rossbeg, following the Wild Atlantic Bay signs. Turn left at the sign for the camping and caravan park and follow this road. **Sheskinmore Nature Reserve** is accessed from a gate and stile along this road, with limited roadside parking. Climb the stile and take the 3km walk through the reserve and dunes to the large, secluded Ballinreavy Strand. For **Tramore Beach** continue past Sheskinmore to the end of this road and the campsite, where there is a small parking area, from which it is a short walk through to the beach.

SCENIC WALK • FAMILY FRIENDLY • NATURE RESERVE • CAMPING AND A SHORT WALK TO THE BEACH

GRID REF: G 68101 95833
GOOGLE MAPS REF:
54.80835, –8.502511

⑦ DOOEY BEACH AND BIG DUNE

The long strand of Dooey Beach in west Donegal feels removed from the rest of the world. The shore shelves gently, making for beautiful swimming while admiring the views across the Gweebarra estuary towards the string of beaches leading to Portnoo and Narin. South along the beach, 'Big Dune' looms out of the grassland – possibly the largest sand dune in Ireland. Rabbits tear through the grass, which in summer is carpeted thickly with daisies. As you trek up Big Dune, the white sand dazzles as it reflects the sun's rays and you are rewarded with spectacular views across the beach and estuary.

After, call in at Elliotts Bar for a refreshing pint before the trip home.

BY CAR: 50 minutes from Donegal town. Take N56 for 9km; turn right onto R262 for 18km; turn right onto N56, then stay on N56 for 15km to Lettermacaward. Turn left and follow the road 5km to the beach.

FAMILY FRIENDLY • SWIMMING AND SURFING

GRID REF: B 75543 02911
GOOGLE MAPS REF:
54.87354, –8.38168

⑧ LEABH BEACH, ÁRAINN MHÓR

Getting to Árainn Mhór involves possibly the nicest ferry journey in Ireland. The ferry passes through a small archipelago of islands with cottages and modernised houses, each with enviable views across to tiny coves and beaches. It is a haven for kayaking: pack a picnic and explore. Arrive at the harbour on Árainn Mhór, where the lovely Leabh Beach beckons you for a swim. At high tide, teens can be found jumping and diving into the clear water from the old slipway. The beach shelves very gently and swimming is possible at all tides. Pop into Teach Phil Ban afterwards for a warming drink and, often, music sessions.

BY CAR and ferry: 12 minute drive from Dungloe, west Donegal, to Burtonport. Take R259 coastal road for 6.7km to Burtonport. Turn left at The Wheelhouse onto R260 down to the pier. The ferry journey is 15 minutes and you can take a car over or travel on foot. There are regular sailings throughout the day. Leabh Beach is a short way from the ferry pier.

FAMILY FRIENDLY • JUMPING AND DIVING • REGULAR FERRY CROSSINGS

GRID REF: B 68340 15583
GOOGLE MAPS REF:
54.98651, –8.49553

Leabh Beach, Árainn Mhór

⑨ ATHPHORT BEACH, ÁRAINN MHÓR

Irish swimmers all over the country will know of octogenarian Paddy Conaghan, who drove all around Ireland's coast, in the winters of 2021/22 and 2022/23, 'ducking' at every pier and beach. Athphort is Paddy's home beach and training ground. The 400m sandy beach curves from rocks below the road to a pier at the far end. Somewhat more exposed than Leabh Beach, it can get choppy. The pier is great for jumping and diving at high water. Keep watch as eddies can form as the tide changes.

BY CAR / on foot: 3km from Leabh Beach. Follow the road up past the two schools to take a sharp right turn. Continue along this road, winding past the community centre. Keep left to stay on the main road and carry on, passing Neily's Bar, open weekends, and Killeens of Arranmore (closed). Here you can see Athphort Beach below. Follow the road down to the beach with a football pitch behind.

FAMILY FRIENDLY • PIER JUMPING • SANDY BEACH

GRID REF: B 66668 13966
GOOGLE MAPS REF:
54.97194, -8.52218

⑩ CRUIT ISLAND BRIDGE

The area from Burtonport to the famous Carrickfinn at Donegal Airport is strewn with beaches galore. Spend a few weeks here and you could swim at a different beach every day! But don't miss out Cruit Island, pronounced 'critch'. It has wild and stormy beaches suitable only for walking, and safe, shallow bays perfect for the family. A favourite spot with locals young and old is the old bridge onto Cruit Island itself. From this the youngsters build their courage to leap into the deep pool below, a rite of passage.

BY CAR: 15 minutes from Dungloe. Take the road to Kincasslagh for 8.5km. Turn left at the Viking House Hotel onto L1463 signed Trá. Pass the school and the road sweeps left, signed Cruit Golf Island Club. Continue to the bridge onto the island.

Be sure to explore the other beaches on Cruit. Out by the golf club is a small harbour where kayaking tours leave to explore Owey Island.

POPULAR JUMPING SPOT • FAMILY FRIENDLY • DEEP WATER

GRID REF: B 73887 18651
GOOGLE MAPS REF:
55.01474, -8.40883

⑪ CARRICKREAGH JETTY

COUNTY FERMANAGH

Swim from this quiet jetty and island-hop in the tranquil waters of Carrickreagh Bay, sheltered on the western shore of Lower Lough Erne south east of the 'Broad Lough'. Take some time to climb the steep trail up through Carrickreagh Wood for fantastic views north to Donegal's Bluestack Mountains and west all the way to Sligo Bay.

The Lough Erne waterways cover a huge area in Fermanagh, where pleasure boaters, holidaymakers and kayakers all enjoy the miles of weaving rivers and lake shore.

Carrickreagh is a small mooring jetty near Ely Lodge Forest on the south-western shore of Lower Lough Erne. Surrounded by trees, this is a picturesque start to a swim.

Moving away from the jetty, follow the depth markers which guide boats through the deep main channel. In the early morning, there should be little traffic but stick to the edge of this channel to keep safely away from any passing boats. Due east from the jetty is a small island, Inish Lougher: swim the short distance across here or perhaps circumnavigate the island, approximately 1¼ miles (2km) around. Just north of Inish Lougher is the even smaller Inish Fovar. If you circumnavigate Lougher, you will see a narrow gap between the two islands almost opposite the jetty. To the north lies the smaller-still Gall Island and it is through the channel between Gall and Fovar that any visiting boats will pass.

Carrickreagh jetty is just along the river from Ely Lodge Forest. The path along the riverbank is popular with walkers. The jetty itself is a short walk along this path from the car park at Ely Lodge. The occasional boat might moor here but this is one of the quiet places on the otherwise busy Erne waterways. Across the road from Carrickreagh, a steep forest track leads up to a viewpoint overlooking Lower Lough Erne all the way to the Bluestack Mountains in Donegal to the north, and Sligo Bay and the Atlantic Ocean to the west. Follow the black route indicated by waymarked posts.

⑭

DONEGAL

⑬

FERMANAGH

Carrickreagh jetty

AT A GLANCE

(11) CARRICKREAGH JETTY
Island-hopping in the sheltered bay south east of Upper Lough Erne (the 'Broad Lough'), a steep forest walk for superb panoramic views, all with easy access and parking close by. Canoeists will find this a great place to launch from and explore the farther islands. Invest in a good map of the area if you plan a canoe tour.

There are picnic tables at the car park (but no other facilities) and easy access to the water off the wooden jetty which has a ladder at either end.

BY CAR: 1 hour 47 minutes from Belfast. Take M1 to Dungannon, then A4 through Fivemiletown to Enniskillen. From here, head for Belleek along A46 Shore Road. Approximately 6 miles (10km) from Enniskillen, Ely Lodge Forest car park is signed and located on the right. Alternatively, continue (about 150 metres) to the Carrickreagh Viewpoint Walk car park on the left. Opposite this is a path through the trees leading to the jetty.

WILD CAMPING • EASY SWIM • PLENTY OF PARKING • BOATS OR CANOES

GRID REF: H 17651 52054
GOOGLE MAPS REF:
54.41674, −7.72895

(12) THRUPENNY POOL AND BUNDORAN BEACH
Thrupenny Pool, so named for the cost of a swim in pre-decimal currency, is a low-walled sea pool which provides a safe haven on rougher days. A small cave to one side provides a sheltered changing area. The shallow, sandy pool allows for paddling and play. Adult swimmers need to be close to the outer wall to get deeper water to complete their laps.

The main beach has rock reefs on either side, with fossils of ancient macrofauna that look like engineered metal parts. Behind the rocks to the right of the town beach is a small cove where a long ladder scales up the rock face to an old diving board plinth, perfect for jumping from at high water.

BY CAR: 26 minutes from Donegal town. Take R267 south to join N15 towards Bundoran. Take R267 into Bundoran town, turn right onto Sea Road where there is a large car park. Walk from here. The town beach is in front, Thrupenny Pool is to the left in front of Waterworld. There are steps and a ramp down to the beach and pool.

TOWN BEACH • LIFEGUARDED IN SUMMER

GRID REF: G 81832 59149
GOOGLE MAPS REF:
54.48064, −8.28117

(13) LOUGH DERG
Across the lough rises the impressive structure of the Sanctuary of St Patrick, dominated by its circular basilica and the great copper dome. For hundreds of years, Station Island was believed to be a special place, even before Saint Patrick arrived in the 12th century. But it was after Patrick's vision of the afterlife during contemplation in a cave here that it became a place of Christian pilgrimage.

The largest lough in Donegal, Lough Derg affords the swimmer plenty of quiet places to explore without interrupting anyone else. Although it would be tempting to swim out to the Sanctuary, they ask that no craft go within 300m of the island. This includes swimmers. Enjoy the tranquillity and admire the grand building from afar.

BY CAR: 35 minutes from Donegal town. Take R267 south for 6km, turn left onto R232 to Pettigo for 21 km. Turn left onto R233 and continue 7km to the Sanctuary car park. Continue along the narrow track to find a quiet spot for your dip.

SECLUDED LAKE SPOT • DEEP WATER • SUITABLE FOR STRONG SWIMMERS ONLY

GRID REF: H 09211 73160
GOOGLE MAPS REF:
54.60668, −7.85689

⑭ GARTAN LOUGH

Beside the entrance gate to Glebe House and Gallery, a narrow concrete lane, a few hundred metres long, brings you to the lough-side pontoon which provides easy access. Swim out through tall reeds towards the small island about 1km away. As you pass the island, the view expands to take in the entire lough. Leave time to visit Glebe House and Gallery, home of renowned artist Derek Hill. It is free to visit the gardens and gallery, or you can book a tour of the house (€5 at the time of writing).

BY CAR: 56 minutes from Donegal town, take N15 north for 28km to Stranorlar. Turn left onto N13. After Drumkeen, turn left onto Treantaboy. After 5km turn left then take the next right towards Roughan. After 1.4km turn left. Cross the bridge and turn left onto R251, then continue onto R250. Crossing the river below Church Hill turn left (signed Gartan/Glebe Gallery). At the gallery take the next left onto the laneway, on to the parking area and the pontoon.

LAKE SWIM WITH PONTOON • ISLAND SWIM

GRID REF: C 06083 17307
GOOGLE MAPS REF:
55.00341, -7.90567

Bundoran

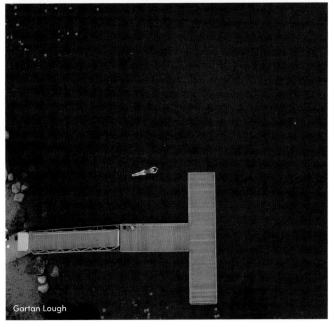

Gartan Lough

⑮ DEVENISH ISLAND

COUNTY FERMANAGH

Swim the short distance from the jetty at Trory Point on the mainland to Devenish jetty to investigate the ruins of an ancient monastic settlement and climb the 30m round tower for remarkable views. Alternatively, swim around the island for a different perspective, crossing the gap known as Friar's Leap, where a holy man is said to have jumped across to escape the devil, who was chasing him after he had broken his vows.

Lough Erne comprises two lakes, the Upper and Lower Loughs, which are joined by a meandering watercourse. Popular with all kinds of water-sports enthusiasts, this inland waterway, stretching from Belleek in the north west to Belturbet in the south east, is studded with islands. For the swimmer there are many spots, either from the riverbanks or along Upper Lough Erne (known as the 'Broad Lough'). Devenish Island, with its religious ruins and sheltered waters, makes for one of the best spots close to Enniskillen.

Plunging in from the wooden jetty at Trory, you may be pleasantly surprised by the warmth of the water. Travelling anticlockwise around the island, take a swim-tour through misadventure and local history. Rounding the southern end of the island, cross Friar's Leap, a stretch of water between Devenish and a small islet just off the mainland. From here, round the south of the island and come to Devenish jetty. A short way north is Trory jetty, our starting point.

Running north/south and at 1¼ miles (2km) long and ⅔ mile (1km) wide, this circumnavigation is a long swim. There is, however, the option of taking a short swim from Trory Point jetty south to Devenish jetty to explore the island. Take a dry bag for clothing or wear a wetsuit and booties.

Be aware that the area is very popular for fishing and boating so make yourself highly visible and keep out of the deeper channels unless accompanied by a canoe or kayak.

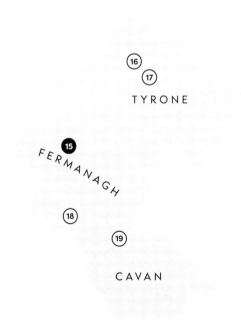

Devenish Island

AT A GLANCE

⑮ DEVENISH ISLAND

Either circumnavigate the island, approximately a 3-mile (5km) swim, or take the short jaunt from Trory Point jetty to Devenish jetty, approximately ½ mile (800m) south and visible from Trory.

BY CAR: 1 hour 25 minutes from Sligo town. Take N16 through Blacklion and Belcoo onto A4 into Enniskillen, then take A32 along the eastern shore of Lough Erne towards Irvinestown for 2 miles (3km). Just before the roundabout at Trory, turn left at the filling station onto a minor road. After ¾ mile (1.2km), take the left fork in the road. The jetty at Trory Point and parking are on the right.

ISLAND SWIM • EASY ACCESS • SOME BOATS

GRID REF: H 22644 47735
GOOGLE MAPS REF:
54.37790, -7.65226

Gortin Lakes

⑯ GORTIN GLEN LAKES

Twin lakes high up above Gortin Glen Forest with a short (1km) walking trail which loops around both lakes; New Lough and Oak Lough, in a figure of eight and gives fantastic views of the Sperrins. New Lough is better for swimming; it gets deep quickly. The lakebed is stony so take care walking in and out. Caution: being high, the lakes get very cold in winter and may freeze, so follow winter swimming advice.

BY CAR: 35 minutes from Omagh. Take A5 north, towards the Folk Park. At the roundabout, take the third exit onto B48/Derry Road; at the next roundabout, take the first exit onto Strathroy Link. Cross the Strule River, then turn right onto Strathroy Road. Go through two roundabouts. At the next roundabout, take the first exit onto B48/Gortin Road. Continue for 12km, passing Gortin Glen Forest, then turn right onto Lenamore Road. The lakes are 800m farther on. Park at New Lough on the right.

SEASONED SWIMMERS • TOILETS AT OAK LOUGH • PARKING AT BOTH • CAUTION IN WINTER

GRID REF: H 49934 84098
GOOGLE MAPS REF:
54.70256, -7.22612

(17) LOUGH MACRORY

At 650m by 450m at its widest, this is a great spot for a dip while the kids are playing football. With plenty of parking, toilets and a café that does great hot chocolate and traybakes, you can take a little time for yourself during those busy weekend runs from sport to sport! The whole area is buzzing with activity and slipping into the lake gives a lovely respite from what could be an otherwise chaotic day. Best advice: keep a swim kit in the car for these opportunities.

BY CAR: 20 minutes from Omagh. Take A5 past the cinema. At the roundabout, take the first exit onto A505. At the next roundabout, take the second exit to stay on A505 for 5 miles (8km). Turn right onto Loughmacrory Road, continue for 3 miles (5km). St Teresa's GAA and the lough parking are on the left.

CAFÉ • TOILETS • PARKING

GRID REF: H 57663 75830
GOOGLE MAPS REF:
54.62776, -7.10807

(18) BRACKLEY LOUGH

Incredibly handy to reach off the N87, the lake is open and, with a small crannóg approximately 400m from the beach, it is popular with local swimmers and triathletes. A line of marker buoys allows for a long loop where stronger swimmers gauge their improvements each time they complete a lap. Nifty wooden bench seating runs the full length of the low fence which demarcates the parking from the sandy beach, providing a place to set your kit off the ground while you swim. Sit here to enjoy your cuppa afterwards. The lake is also used for fishing and occasionally small boats will launch from the slip to the right of the beach area.

BY CAR: 35 minutes from Cavan town. Take N3 north for 20km. At the roundabout, take the first exit onto N87 and continue for 20km. Brackley Lough parking is on the left.

FAMILY FRIENDLY • GOOD FOR DISTANCE TRAINING • PARKING AND TOILETS • FISHING LAKE

GRID REF: H 19652 21280
GOOGLE MAPS REF:
54.14024, -7.70038

(19) ANNAGH LOUGH

This pretty lough has been a popular bathing area for many years and doesn't disappoint. Just off the N3 near Butler's Bridge, it is incredibly easy to find. From the wooden changing rooms, a wood-chip path leads down to the small sandy beach which gently shelves to swimming depth. Here, during the summer months, Irish Water Safety volunteers run children's swimming lessons. Perfect for a range of swimmers. Nervous swimmers can stay close to the beach and picnic area – and within their depth! – while accomplished swimmers may want to venture farther into the lake for a longer swim. As Annagh is also a wildfowl sanctuary, you may be lucky enough to spot some interesting visitors during your swim!

BY CAR: 35 minutes from Enniskillen. Take A4/Sligo Road. At the roundabout, turn left onto A509 for 27km. Continue onto N3 for 9.5km. Turn right to the lakeside parking.

FAMILY FRIENDLY • CHANGING ROOMS • MARKER BUOYS • HEIGHT RESTRICTION ON CAR PARK WITH LAY-BY PARKING OPPOSITE

GRID REF: H 39730 12777
GOOGLE MAPS REF:
54.06231, -7.39462

⑳ KINNAGOE

COUNTY DONEGAL

The Inishowen 100 scenic route passes Kinnagoe Bay, with its deep golden sands and three separate beaches. The first beach is claimed by many to be the most beautiful in Ireland. Here, divers regularly come to seek artefacts from the wreck of the Armada ship *La Trinidad Valencera*, which was lost in 1588. The wreck was discovered in 1971.

The first view of the stunning beach from the top of the hill on this scenic route raises the heart rate in excitement. The road drops steeply down as you weave around each corner (there are widened lay-bys for passing vehicles), impatient to reach your destination.

At the shore there is a large, tarmacked parking area. The beach stretches out to the right with sand so deep and soft you sink to your ankles. Kick off your shoes and wade on this popular beach where, in the summer, some families will pitch their tents and remain for weeks on end.

The beach is large so there is plenty of space. Swim in the clear waters and snorkel around the rocks in search of Armada treasure but for more privacy, walk the length of the strand to a narrow track that climbs up and over the rocks to a second, quieter bay. Few come this far so you may well have this beach to yourself. The sand is still deep and soft. Search for shells washed up on shore and enjoy the solitude.

Halfway along this bay, an area of long grass bridges the gap between the foliage-dense hillside and the sand; a river runs out to the sea. Press through this thick grass upstream a few hundred metres to a small waterfall and a shallow bathing pool. The dark water spilling over the rocks fizzles as it is aerated, creamy-white foam pouring into an inky pool.

At the far end of this bay another track leads up and over the rocks into a third, even more secluded bay. Here you can be alone, with only the wheeling birds and the swish of the sea for company. A quiet spot for those inclined to skinny-dip.

DONEGAL

RIGHT Kinnagoe Bay

AT A GLANCE

20 KINNAGOE

Sink ankle deep in the soft sands of the three strands at Kinnagoe Bay, on the north-eastern shore of the Inishowen Peninsula, approximately 10km from Moville. Camp on the first and most popular beach or cross the strand and follow a narrow track over the rocks to the second, quieter bay; an even more secluded third cove lies over a second headland, approximately twenty minutes' walk from the first beach.

BY CAR: 50 minutes from Derry/ Londonderry city. Take A2 north, then follow R238 along the shore of Lough Foyle to Moville. Turn left onto R238/Main St, continue for 5km. Turn right (signed Kinnagoe Bay), then turn right (signed Glenagivney) and continue for 5.5km. Turn left down the narrow, winding road to the beach parking.

SCENIC WALK • FAMILY FRIENDLY • BEACH CAMPING

GRID REF: C 62832 46114
GOOGLE MAPS REF:
55.25843, -7.01289

21 PORTNABLAGH

The home of Gartan Open Water Swimmers (a very sociable bunch, so if you want to meet up message them on Facebook), Portnablagh has a nice little beach tucked in beside the harbour and you can swim from either the beach or the harbour slipway itself, boat traffic dependent. With the broad stretch of Killahoey Beach opposite, there are plenty of swim options.

Gartan Open Water Swimmers also run charity swims throughout the year and strong swimmers may want to get in touch for a trip around to the blowhole – over a mile trip which needs perfect conditions!

BY CAR: 30 minutes from Letterkenny. Take N56 north for 32km, then turn left down to the beach and harbour. Parking on the roadside or at the harbour slip.

FAMILY FRIENDLY • POPULAR • ORGANISED SWIMS YEAR ROUND

GRID REF: C 04629 37124
GOOGLE MAPS REF:
55.18144, -7.92810

22 CULDAFF

Culdaff sits high on the Inishowen Peninsula on the R238 between Moville and Carndonagh. This well-tended village has a series of holiday homes and plenty of pubs and eateries (check out McGrory's around the corner on the main street where they serve food all day). The strand here is nice with several smaller coves off the main beach at the opposite end to the harbour. A good children's play park sits on the dune just above the beach. This is becoming more popular with families and holidaymakers.

BY CAR: 45 minutes from Derry/ Londonderry, take A515 across the Foyle Bridge, then turn right heading for Muff. Continue on R238, passing St Columba's church and the garage. Turn left onto L1441 for 1.5km. Turn left, signed Gleneely, and after 4.5km turn left onto L1411. Continue through Gleneely and onto R238 for 4.5km, then turn right down towards Culdaff Shore Road.

FAMILY FRIENDLY • POPULAR

GRID REF: C 54275 49879
GOOGLE MAPS REF:
55.29335, -7.14824

Culdaff

23 LENANKEEL BEACH AND THE POITÍN REPUBLIC OF URRIS

This quiet beach is used mainly by locals, with a small fishing pier to the right and the craggy outline of the Urris Mountains to the left.

The beach is gently shelving and the water beautifully clear. Swim the 600m across the bay towards the fishing pier or explore along the left-hand shoreline under the shadow of the mountains, for small caves. The area is a local favourite, with signage guiding you to several walks of interest in the area, two of which lead from the beach, one 2.5km, the other 6.5km, over the Urris Hills.

The Poitín Republic of Urris: it's well worth taking a drive, very steep cycle or walk up over the Mamore Gap for superb views back across the Inishowen Peninsula. In 1811, poitín – illegal whiskey – was being produced in large quantities here and the parish was ordered to pay a substantial fine; rather than pay this, the people of Urris declared a republic and the flat land below the gap remained independent until 1815.

BY CAR: 1 hour from Derry/Londonderry. Head north and take R238 through Buncrana to Clonmany. Follow Wild Atlantic Way (S) for 6.5km. Keep right at the fork. After 1.5km the road sweeps round to the left. Continue to the little hamlet and park on the roadside near the beach.

FAMILY FRIENDLY • LIMITED PARKING

GRID REF: C 30706 43714
GOOGLE MAPS REF:
55.23961, -7.51804

24 FORT DUNREE PIER AND BEACH

This popular military museum has some amazing views across Lough Swilly to the broad strands of Ballymastocker Bay. Take the time to wander around the fort grounds, then climb down to the narrow slipway and pier where there are steps leading into the deep water – this would be an overlooked swim but it's fun on a calm day to view the fort from beneath the cliff. Best for strong swimmers. Up at the fort again, walk the path past the lighthouse and on around the headland and you'll see Dunree Beach below.

The beach access is through a small parking area on the roadside north of the fort. Climb the stile and take the sandy path through the grasslands down to the pretty beach. Explore the coastline for caves, swim around to the right, under the Urris hills to a second, smaller beach near the point of this sheltered bay.

BY CAR: 15 minutes from Buncrana. Take R238 for 1.8km. Turn left onto Gleann Aibhinn for 8km, then left up to the fort.

FAMILY FRIENDLY BEACH SWIM • PIER SWIM SUITABLE FOR STRONG SWIMMERS ONLY

GRID REF: C 28508 38899
GOOGLE MAPS REF:
55.19668, -7.55275

㉕ DUNAGREE POINT

COUNTY DONEGAL

Follow the road out of Moville towards Inishowen Head and stop at almost any hole in the hedge to park your car or bike on the roadside. Peek through that gap and you will probably find a cove or tiny beach, completely deserted. With a coastal walk, rocks to dive from and two beaches at which to swim, Dunagree is a gem, with camping space on both beaches. With the Atlantic swell washing into this little bay, you can play in the surf or swim out beyond the breakers, or venture around the lighthouse to the smaller beach. Finish the day with a barbecue and listen to the waves as evening light descends.

Dunagree Lighthouse sits in private gardens flanked by two beaches: the first, small and sheltered with soft white sand quickly shelving into deep water, tends to be deserted, visitors preferring the handy car parking of the second, larger beach. The car park is basic, a rectangle of tarmac with two Portaloos to the side. A lifeguard hut perches on the dune above the beach. There is a quaint old-fashionedness about it all. The lighthouse sits above the dunes to the right of the bay and, to the left, the rough and craggy rocks carry an old concrete bridge, which beckons to the explorer.

From these rocks a shoreline track leads around to 'the Arch', which locals promise you will know when you see it, and you will. Follow the rough track from the beach, passing several inlets and rocky coves where you could swim, but continue to the Arch, which is a special, secret place.

Trainers rather than sandals are recommended for pushing through the tall bracken. Continue until the path drops back down onto the shore, climb over the occasional large rock, and then you will see it: just as the path turns the corner, a high cliff juts out from the shore into the sea, blocking the path save for the Arch, a low doorway through the wall. Step through into the ancient amphitheatre of St Columba's Cove. This quiet place could awaken wonders of the imagination!

DONEGAL

RIGHT Dunagree Point

AT A GLANCE

25 DUNAGREE POINT

Beach camping, a rugged coastal path and swimming as the sun goes down, on either of the two beaches. Camping is possible on either beach: the smaller is accessed through a field where a little byre houses a few cattle, fenced off from the strand. Pitch up anywhere along this shoreline above the high-water mark. The larger beach might be preferable, being closer to the Portaloos. To the left of the track that leads from the car park onto the sand, a low wall of rock provides shelter from wind and prying eyes.

BY CAR: 70 minutes from Derry/Londonderry city, take A2 to Muff and then R238 along the shores of Lough Foyle, through Moville. From there, take R241 through Greencastle towards Stroove. Dunagree is the last beach before the road loops back on itself at Inishowen Head.

BEACH CAMPING • SCENIC WALK • FAMILY FRIENDLY

GRID REF: C 68255 42693
GOOGLE MAPS REF:
55.22729, -6.92804

26 INCH ISLAND PIER

With views across this lower end of Lough Swilly to Lisfannon Beach to the east and the very popular Rathmullan on the western shore, this quiet pier and beach are a haven away from the crowds. With deep water, you can dive from the pier or, if you prefer, wade in from the small beach. Shaded under the tree canopy, enjoy the peace of this quiet spot.

While you're here, check out the 8km loop walk from the wildlife reserve which takes you across the second embankment made by the Lough Swilly Railway in 1855.

BY CAR: 30 minutes from Derry/Londonderry. Take A2/Buncrana Road north to Bridge End (10km). At the roundabout, take the second exit onto A238 for 2.7km, then turn left onto Inch Road. Crossing onto the island, turn right and continue for 1.6km. Turn right and continue for another 1.6km. Turn right again and follow the road down to the tiny beach and pier.

BEACH SWIM • PIER JUMPING AT HIGH WATER • FAMILY FRIENDLY

GRID REF: C 31050 26367
GOOGLE MAPS REF:
55.083848, -7.51459

27 BALLYMASTOCKER BEACH

With almost 3km of strand, it's no wonder this is a go-to holiday destination. It also means there's plenty of room to find your own space. The bay shelves gently so is perfect for all swimming abilities, although in strong winds there can be quite the surf.

Take the steep, winding road up the mountainside for the best photo op from the viewpoint above the bay. East facing, the strand can get exposed but that makes it all the more beautiful. Keep to this southern end of the beach for quiet under the mountain slopes.

BY CAR: 35 minutes from Letterkenny. Take N56 for 4.7km and then turn right onto L1352 for 10km. Turn left onto R245. Turn right onto R246 and continue for 12km, then turn right. Turn left at Knockalla Cottages and continue to the beach parking.

POPULAR FAMILY-FRIENDLY BEACH • TOILETS • PARKING

GRID REF: C 24943 38183
GOOGLE MAPS REF:
55.18919, -7.60862

Trá Na Rosann

㉘ TRÁ NA ROSANN

You are spoilt for choice for beautiful beaches on the popular Rosguill peninsula. As you arrive at the holiday resort of Downings, the curved beach sits below the town. To the south is the long strand of Tramore but make your way north, following the loop road to Trá na Rosann (still a popular spot, with a caravan park, but less crowded than Downings). From the parking area, it's a 200m sandy track to the beach. When the tide is low you can walk around the headland under Glenoory to a second beach. Be sure to return before the tide cuts you off or it's a steep trek over the hill.

BY CAR: 45 minutes from Letterkenny. Take N56 north for 10.6km. Turn right, signed Lough Salt and Lough Keel. After 1km turn left and continue for 14km, joining R245. Turn left onto R248 onto the peninsula and continue for 5.8km before turning right. After 1km, turn left up to Trá na Rosann.

POPULAR • FAMILY FRIENDLY

GRID REF: C 11787 42059
GOOGLE MAPS REF:
55.22470, –7.81435

㉙ LUCKY SHELL BEACH, ARDS FOREST AND FRIARY

Walk the path to the right of Ards Friary and, as you turn the corner, the first beach comes into view: St Catherine's Beach. Although this spot looks tempting for a swim, it is dangerous, with strong currents and soft, sinking sand. Carry on along the coastal path as it rises past a series of narrow inlets, topped with purple heather. Keep walking along this track and, as you round the headland, you come to the beautiful Lucky Shell Beach. Make your way down the steep, sometimes slippery track to the beach and allow your feet to sink into coarse golden sand, the crumbs of thousands of shells clinging to your toes as you walk along this carpet sweeping into crystal-clear water.

BY CAR: 37 minutes from Letterkenny. Take N56 north, through Creeslough (27.5km). Turn right at Doe Cemetery, signed Ards Friary. Turn right again, and continue 4.5km to the friary.

PARKING • GIFT SHOP • TOILETS

GRID REF: C 09035 35319
GOOGLE MAPS REF:
55.16578, –7.85951

㉚ DUNSEVERICK HARBOUR AND SLOUGH

COUNTY ANTRIM

Climb the rocks to plunge from various heights into this little-known gem on the north coast. The Slough at Dunseverick is a cleft cut in the rocks, forming a deep inlet perfect for jumping and diving, being narrow and sheltered from the North Atlantic. The black rocks provide plenty of diving platforms. Here, young folk aim to dive through the centre of a giant inflatable ring from a height while others lounge on neon-bright lilos, shouting encouragement. A mix of wetsuited and swimsuited explorers challenge themselves to ever-higher jumps and dives.

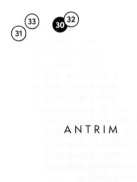

ANTRIM

On the coast road between Ballintoy and Bushmills, Dunseverick could easily be missed, but take the single-track road towards the shore, signed for Dunseverick Harbour, and park along the verge. The Slough is found by climbing over the wooden stile on the roadside, which leads through a field ablaze with yellow gorse from spring. The grass gives way to rocks until you stumble across the narrow cleft in the rocks, sheltered from the worst of the Atlantic swell. On one side of this deep, narrow inlet, small patches of sand provide natural picnic sites, sheltered from the breeze between the large rocks. On the other side you can spend hours clambering, jumping and diving, warming yourself with the heat from the rocks.

For those who want a longer swim, the picturesque Dunseverick Harbour at the end of the narrow road is a good place to park. From here, walk into crystal-clear waters between the two jetties and marvel at the variety of colours of kelp and other seaweeds as large fish cruise beneath, oblivious to your presence; the perfect spot for snorkelling.

In calm conditions, it is possible to swim from here to the Slough: swim out from the harbour and turn left between the two large rocks. Follow the shoreline to the Slough about 750m away. The swell of the North Atlantic gives this the feeling of a wild adventure swim; even with no breakers, the gentle swell of the water can seem like the sea is breathing quietly but with immense underlying power.

Jumping at the Slough

AT A GLANCE

30 DUNSEVERICK

The Slough at Dunseverick provides a sheltered inlet for lazing away long summer days: jumping, diving, plunging and picnicking. Strong swimmers may want to swim from the petite Dunseverick Harbour along the rugged coastline and into the shelter of the Slough. This is for strong, competent swimmers as, while it is not a long swim, the tides here are strong. The Slough, though, is suitable for many levels of swimmer. The North Atlantic is cold with strong swells, so know your limitations and always swim safe.

BY CAR: 1 hour 20 minutes from Belfast. Take M2 north. At Junction 1 take A26 and continue towards Antrim, Ballymena, Coleraine. After approx. 12 miles (19km), turn right onto A44 to Ballycastle. Take B15 coast road to Ballintoy. Follow signposts for the Giant's Causeway and then Dunseverick Harbour. Park at Dunseverick Harbour car park.

BY BUS: the Causeway Rambler Bus runs during summer between Bushmills and Carrick-a-Rede.

FAMILY FRIENDLY • ROCK POOLS • JUMPING WITH CARE • STRONG SWIMMERS ONLY OUTSIDE HARBOUR

GRID REF: C 99979 44510
GOOGLE MAPS REF:
55.23748, -6.42869

31 PORTSTEWART STRAND

Walk the scenic and vertiginous coastal path from the promenade to Portstewart Strand. There are dunes and 2 miles (3km) of sandy beach to explore from this cliff path to the River Bann. The path has panoramic views across the strand and Downhill with Donegal in the distance. A popular beach with areas for watersports and great for family days out.

BY CAR: 1 hour 20 minutes from Belfast. Take M2 north. At Junction 1 take A26/Antrim. Continue on A26, taking M2 ring road around Ballymena and back onto A26. Approaching Ballymoney, at the roundabout, take the second exit onto A26/Frosses Road. At the roundabout, take the third exit onto B62/Ballybogey Road. Continue for 4 miles (6.5km), then turn left onto B67/Ballyrashane Road. At the roundabout, take the third exit onto A29. At the next roundabout, take the first exit and then right onto Cromore Road. After 1 mile (1.6km), turn left onto Agherton Road. At Burnside roundabout, take the first exit onto Burnside Road and continue to Strand Road and the beach. Paid parking on the beach.

TOILETS • CHANGING • BEACH SHOWERS • SHOP • CAFÉ

GRID REF: C 81066 36691
GOOGLE MAPS REF:
55.17120, -6.72876

32 BALLINTOY HARBOUR

The road winds steeply down in a series of switchbacks to this lovely old harbour. Popular as a section of the Causeway Coast walk, it is also a destination for *Game of Thrones* fans as the location where Theon Greyjoy returned to the Iron Islands. Craggy coves to the left of the harbour display some awesome sea stacks and arches. And you can see why, a few hundred years ago, this area was known for smuggling. You have a choice of swim spots: the harbour itself is sheltered, there is a small, shallow beach to the left and, at the corner above the harbour, there is a track leading down to two more little beaches. Climbing back up to the main Causeway Road check out the curious Bendhu House with its variety of windows designed to capture each and every view.

BY CAR: 15 minutes from Ballycastle. Take B15/Clare Road west. Turning right onto Whitepark Road, continue for 4.5 miles (7.5km), passing Carrick-a-Rede rope bridge, to Ballintoy village. Turn right onto Harbour Road.

TOILETS • COASTAL WALKS • BEACH AND HARBOUR SWIM • POPULAR • PARKING AT THE HARBOUR.

GRID REF: D 03756 45303
GOOGLE MAPS REF:
55.24423, -6.36936

Ballintoy Harbour beach

㉝ ARCADIA BEACH

Portrush is a bustling, lively town with a variety of surf schools.
Set on a little peninsula it has two main beaches with the tiny Arcadia Beach nestled between. The large east strand beside Arcadia has several miles of sand with good surf and the smaller west bay, beside Portrush Harbour, is more sheltered. Both beaches are popular for swimming and surfing.

Eastwards along the coast, you will see the ruins of Dunluce Castle, thought to be the inspiration for Cair Paravel in C.S. Lewis' *Chronicles of Narnia*. On a misty morning it has a magical quality.

BY CAR: 1 hour 20 minutes from Belfast. Take M2 north. At Junction 1 take the A26/Antrim. Continue on A26, taking M2 ring road around Ballymena and back onto A26. Approaching Ballymoney, at the roundabout, take the second exit onto A26/Frosses Road. At the roundabout, take the third exit onto B62/Ballybogey Road. Continue for 16km to Dunluce Road, then turn left towards Portrush. There is a car park at east strand and you can see Arcadia Café to the left.

CAFÉS • FAMILY FRIENDLY • POPULAR

GRID REF: C 85936 40670
GOOGLE MAPS REF:
55.20579, -6.65081

❸❹ CARRICK-A-REDE

COUNTY ANTRIM

Swim in clear turquoise waters across Larrybane Bay past rugged white cliffs to the tiny island of Carrick-a-Rede. Swim under the narrow rope bridge high above and move into the deeper waters to the east of the island, with cliffs rising up all around.

A rough track curves down from the old quarry below the main car park at Carrick-a-Rede and the path leading to the rope bridge. As you turn the corner, the first views of Sheep Island appear to the west, where strong currents swirl the water into eddies.

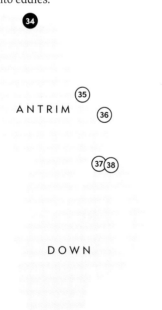

A line of calm water can be seen between here and the sheltered Larrybane Bay. On the shore, white chalky cliffs stretch up from huge boulders which, in turn, melt into pale sand beneath the turquoise sea. The high grass-topped island, tethered to the mainland by the rope bridge, is a picturesque scene.

Carrick-a-Rede Island sits only a short distance from shore but high cliffs make it inaccessible to walk to from the land. Now managed by the National Trust, the rope bridge draws thousands of visitors in the summer.

For swimmers the opportunity to view the bridge from a different angle is the reward of a scramble over the rocks at Larrybane, followed by the long swim across the bay. Swim to the island and through the narrow gap between it and the shore, swimming beneath the rope bridge. This is a good 1 mile (2km) round trip.

Beyond the bridge, great black cliffs soar upwards and the shallow caves amplify the sound of the waves. A set of steep steps leads down from the tiny fisherman's cottage, past a broken and rusting winch, a remnant of the old salmon fishery.

Return under the bridge across this picturesque bay to climb out and scramble back up over the rocks.

ABOVE AND LEFT
Carrick-a-Rede

AT A GLANCE

34 CARRICK-A-REDE

From Larrybane Bay, swim beneath the Carrick-a-Rede rope bridge to the old salmon fisheries. This is an advanced swim for the experienced open-water swimmer. It requires knowledge of both the swimmer's limitations and the local tides.

It is wise to avoid the bay to the west of Sheep Island as here the currents are much stronger and the eddies can be powerful.

BY CAR: 1 hour 15 minutes from Belfast/10 minutes from the Giant's Causeway. From Belfast take M2 north through Ballymena, then A26, turning onto A44 to Ballycastle. Take B15 coast road towards Ballintoy and Carrick-a-Rede. Drive through the main car park and down to the overspill car park in the quarry. Leave the car here and follow the track on foot to the shore. Sandals are recommended.

BY BUS: the Ulster Bus Causeway Rambler service runs between Bushmills and Carrick-a-Rede during the summer. Check with Ulster Bus for timetables.

SECLUDED • SEA CAVES • DIFFICULT PATH • ADVENTURE SWIM • ROCKS AND HAZARDS • STRONG SWIMMERS ONLY

GRID REF: D 06106 44854
GOOGLE MAPS REF:
55.24241, -6.35107

35 BALLYGALLY BEACH

Perfect for families and all levels of swimmer, this sandy area is close to the road and car parking. Grey seals and otters have been seen here searching for food. The main entrance to the beach is directly opposite the shop following a short, sloping path to a wooden platform. About 100m from this is a set of steps. Ballygally Beach stretches for 200m in front of the 17th-century Ballygally Castle Hotel, reputed to be one of the most haunted places in Ulster. After your swim, grab a hot chocolate or coffee and perhaps visit the ghost room up in the castle turret.

BY CAR: 40 minutes from Belfast. Take M2 north for 4.5 miles (7km). At Junction 4, take A8/A4 exit Larne/Glengormley. At Sandyknowes roundabout, take the fourth exit onto A8. Continue on A8 through three roundabouts, for 20 miles (32km). Take the exit B148/Cairncastle/Millbrook and continue onto Drumaho Road for 0.5 miles (1km), then right onto Ballyhampton Road. Keep left onto Ballymuck Road and continue for 2.5 miles (4km). Turn right onto Croft Road and continue 1.5 miles (2.5km) to Ballygally sea front.

POPULAR • FAMILY FRIENDLY

GRID REF: D 37239 07836
GOOGLE MAPS REF:
54.89881, -5.85873

Ballygally

Portmuck

Helen's Bay

(36) PORTMUCK

North of Belfast city and through the ancient town of Carrickfergus along the coast road, take a side trip to the pretty Islandmagee.

Quiet country roads and breathtaking scenery are the offerings of this tiny peninsula, perfect for cyclists. Once a haven for smugglers, Portmuck is now a serene sight. Whitewashed cottages sit high on the cliffs, overlooking the old-fashioned harbour. The harbour is sheltered on both sides from the battering of the North Channel by tall cliffs and this natural cove is further protected from the strong tides by the nearby Isle of Muck, or Pig Island. There are strong currents around Pig Island.

Several walks lead up over the cliffs from the harbour and provide terrific views across to Scotland.

BY CAR: travelling north from Belfast city on the A2 towards Larne, turn right onto the B90 then take the B150, following the signs to Portmuck. The road to the harbour is narrow, winding and steep and the final hill affords a wonderful view across to Pig Island.

SCENIC WALK • FAMILY FRIENDLY • BOATS OR CANOES • POPULAR

GRID REF: D 46008 02353
GOOGLE MAPS REF:
54.84729, -5.72745

(37) HELEN'S BAY

Helen's Bay is a very popular beach on the coastal path that runs from Holywood through to Bangor. At any time of day, you are sure to find swimmers of all ages enjoying the sheltered bay. You can swim at any tide time and there are marker buoys set at 100m distances, at time of writing. A super training ground for distance swimmers, the beach is 400m long so is perfect for laps. There is a train halt at Helen's Bay but at weekends during the summer it can be closed due to overcrowding.

BY CAR: 20 minutes from Belfast. Take A2 towards Airport/Bangor/Holywood. Continue for 8 miles (12.5km), past the airport and Holywood. Turn left at Craigdarragh Road. The car park is 1 mile (2km) down this residential area on the right. Walk to the beach. The car park closes at 9 p.m. in summer and 7 p.m. in winter.

VERY POPULAR BEACH NEAR THE CITY • FAMILY FRIENDLY • COASTAL PATH • TOILETS AT CAR PARK

GRID REF: J 46013 82906
GOOGLE MAPS REF:
54.67317, -5.73719

(38) JENNY WATT'S COVE

Take a dip where Bangor's lady smuggler would hide her loot.

The little cove at Brompton has a rich history both of smuggling and swimming. Opposite the old pier, you can see the opening to a small cave, and on a calm day you can swim inside. The whole area is rocky and has a wealth of sea life so it attracts divers and, in recent years, more sea swimmers. Marker buoys have been set up for various distances. This is an exposed area with tricky access down a metal ladder. **Do not swim in rough conditions.**

BY CAR: 30 minutes from Belfast. Take A2 towards Airport/Bangor/Holywood. Continue for 12 miles (19km). Turn left onto Springfield Road. At the roundabout, take the second exit onto B20/Crawfordsburn Road. At the next roundabout, take the second exit onto Maxwell Road. After 0.5 mile (600m) turn left onto Downshire Road, then right onto Brompton Road.

LIMITED ROADSIDE PARKING • CALM CONDITIONS ONLY • ACCESS AND EGRESS VIA A STEEP METAL LADDER

GRID REF: J 49421 82408
GOOGLE MAPS REF:
54.66777, -5.68453

39 BENDERG BAY AND LECALE WAY

COUNTY DOWN

Two for one at this sheltered coastline: first, walk through the grasslands of Killard Nature Reserve to Benderg Beach, home to sand martins and seals. Perfect on a sunny day for swimming, picnicking and investigating the rock pools. The more adventurous will enjoy walking the Lecale Way shoreline track from Ballyhornan, past Gun Island and on to the cleft in the rocks at Benboy Hill for jumping and diving.

From Strangford, the Lecale Way follows the County Down coastline for 31 miles (50km) along quiet roads, past beaches and on coastal paths, all the way to the ancient dune system of Murlough Bay, Ireland's first nature reserve.

South of Strangford and just outside the mouth of Strangford Lough lies Killard Nature Reserve and the secluded Benderg Bay. This superb strand stretches just over half a kilometre from the rocks of Killard Point to the sand cliffs and farmland that separate Benderg from its more popular neighbour, Ballyhornan Beach.

At Mill Quarter Bay, the strength of Strangford Lough's tidal run creates whirlpools in the swift-moving water. This is not the place to swim. A 20-minute walk from here through the nature reserve leads to Benderg. Tucked away behind Killard Point, the beach is sheltered from the tidal race and you can swim in crystal-clear shallow waters. The rocks to the left of the beach teem with life, including young seals hunting for crabs.

Spend a lazy day picnicking and swimming or scramble along the rough coastline south to Ballyhornan Beach. At the far end of Ballyhornan a narrow trail leads along the Lecale Way coastal path to Ardglass. About half an hour's walk along this path brings you to a superb inlet for jumping and diving. The path rises steeply up to a rickety wooden stile and then a sweeping curve above the inlet. To reach the water, scramble down the steep grass banks and then onto the rocks on either side of this inlet. Take care climbing down and watch the tides to ensure you can climb out again. This is one for strong swimmers.

RIGHT Inlet, Lecale Way coastal path

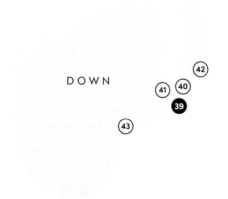

DOWN

42

41 40

39

43

AT A GLANCE

㊴ BENDERG BAY AND LECALE WAY

Benderg Bay is a secluded beach of pale sand, stretching half a kilometre behind Killard Nature Reserve. This gently shelving bay provides a great swim or dip. Alternatively, walk the Lecale Way for quiet inlets and coves for the excitement of a great wild swim. A good walk is followed by a rock climb and swim, great for jumping and exploring. Keep a good eye on water levels to ensure a safe exit.

Take the car ferry from Strangford to Portaferry to witness the strong currents and visit the aquarium for a great family day out.

Kilclief beach

BY CAR: 7 minutes from Strangford. Take A2 Shore Road out of Strangford. At Kilclief, veer left towards Mill Quarter Bay. Park at the roadside lay-by from where signs point to the track leading to Killard Nature Reserve. Follow the path past the mouth of Strangford Lough. The rough track cuts through farmland and onto Benderg Bay. It is a twenty-minute walk to beach.

ROADSIDE PARKING • NO FACILITIES • SCENIC WALK • FAMILY FRIENDLY • SECLUDED • SNORKELLING • ROCK POOLS • ADVENTURE SWIM •

GRID REF: J 60722 43067
GOOGLE MAPS REF:
54.31206, -5.53239

㊵ KILCLIEF BEACH

A small cove, hemmed in by rocks on either side and with a small rock outcrop in the centre, a beautifully protected little bay at the mouth of Strangford Lough. The sand is fine and white, and the beach shelves quickly to a nice swimming depth. The rocks on either side are home to plenty of sea life, so bring a mask and snorkel to explore and watch your toes as velvet and brown crabs stand guard over their hunting grounds on the seabed. Behind is the tower house of Kilclief Castle, built between 1413 and 1441 by the Bishop of Down. Stay within the confines of the 100m-wide cove, safe from the fast-flowing tides of Strangford Lough.

BY CAR: 5 minutes from Strangford village along the A2/Shore Road. Pass the GAC. Around the corner is the small parking area at Kilclief.

POPULAR IN SUMMER • GREAT SWIM SPOT YEAR-ROUND • NO FACILITIES

GRID REF: J 59797 45792
GOOGLE MAPS REF:
54.33579, -5.54367

41 LOUGH MONEY

Filled with water lilies blooming in the spring, the picturesque Lough Money is a quiet haven, 1km long and only 250m at its widest. Step in at the slipway and meander through the deeper waters along the centre line of the lake. This is a fishing lake and also used by triathletes and swimmers. Swans are common and you can hear the gentle *wap, wap, wap* of their wingtips hitting the water as they beat to take flight.

BY CAR: 10 minutes from Downpatrick. Take B1/Ardglass Road past Down Hospital. Continue onto Ballyhornan Road for 2 miles (3km). At Ballyalton, take the left-hand fork, signed Lough Money. It is 1 mile (1.5km) to the lough.

FISHING AND SWIMMING LAKE • STRONG SWIMMERS ONLY

GRID REF: J 53235 45187
GOOGLE MAPS REF:
54.332458, -5.64477

42 KNOCKINELDER

When exploring the Ards Peninsula take some time at Knockinelder Beach. If you are here early enough, you may see some local horses being introduced to the sea in the morning sun. From here you can walk along the coastal path to the National Trust cottages at Kearney, or, at the south end of the beach, discover several more coves leading towards the impressive Quintin Castle. Beyond the castle is Ballyquintin Nature Reserve at the southern tip of the peninsula. With rare wildflowers and a plethora of birdlife, this reserve is worth a visit.

When the wind picks up, Knockinelder gets some good waves and there is a chance that you'll share the water with the occasional kitesurfer.

BY CAR: 45 minutes from Comber. Take A21 to Newtownards. At the roundabouts, follow A20/Portaferry Road. Continue down the Ards Peninsula for 19 miles (30km). Turn left onto Ballyblack Road and after 2 miles (3km) reach Knockinelder Beach. There is parking at either end of the beach.

FAMILY FRIENDLY • SWIMMING • KITESURFING

GRID REF: J 63550 51231
GOOGLE MAPS REF:
54.38401, -5.48211

43 MURLOUGH BAY

This 3-mile (5km) sand and pebble beach is backed by an ancient dune system with great views of Newcastle and the Mourne Mountains. Explore the boardwalks through the 6,000-year-old sand dunes of Murlough Nature Reserve, which is excellent for swimming, walking and birdwatching. Leaving the car at Twelve Arches, you have half a mile (1km) of boardwalk to the beach. Stretching 3 miles (5km) from Dundrum estuary to Newcastle, there is plenty of room to get away from the crowds. The best area to swim is towards the Dundrum (north) end of the beach around high tide.

At the National Trust car park, Newcastle, there is a picnic area, café, toilets. Lifeguarded during the bathing season.

BY CAR: 5 minutes from Newcastle to parking then a 10-minute walk through dunes to beach. Situated off A2 Newcastle–Clough road, 3 miles (5km) from Newcastle and 3 miles (5km) from Clough. The National Trust car park is signposted from A2. There is also roadside car parking at Twelve Arches just outside Dundrum.

FAMILY FRIENDLY • WALKING • SAND DUNES

GRID REF: J 400335
GOOGLE MAPS REF:
54.23530 -5.86326

㊹ JANET'S ROCK

COUNTY DOWN

Swim in the crystal-clear water of a sheltered bay with a myriad of seaweed colours on the rocky floor where fish hide in crevices and tiny crabs scuttle. Then climb barefoot and explore the rock pools to the left of the cove. Search for tiny sea creatures or glide underwater through a narrow gap in the rocks from one pool to another.

The A2 coastal road from Newcastle in County Down, travelling south, goes through Ballymartin and Kilkeel, all the way to Carlingford Lough and the pretty village of Rostrevor.

With the Mourne Mountains rising up to one side and the road hugging the coast, many narrow lanes lead down to the shore where hidden beaches, known only to locals, provide some superb swimming. At Ballymartin, halfway between Annalong and Kilkeel, Janet's Rock is easy to find, and has a bus stop close to the top of the laneway.

The steep, rough track drops down from the road to the shore, revealing the small cove. It is a perfectly contained bathing area. The rocky outcrop to the left of the sandy beach gives its name to the spot – Janet's Rock. This sheltered bay quickly gets to a good depth for swimming. In the shallows, you may have to step over rocks before reaching deep water.

Janet's Rock has pools to explore, some large enough to swim in, and at the point farthest out, when the tide is high, you can dive from these rocks into the bay.

Several lobster pots lie moored a little way outside the cove and seals are often seen. It has been known as a place where seals will hunt in groups, chasing the fish and corralling them in the small bay.

A world away from the busy strand at Cranfield, south of Kilkeel, Janet's Rock will often be entirely deserted, with perhaps the occasional fisher heading out to check their lobster pots.

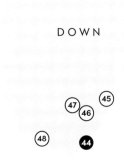

DOWN

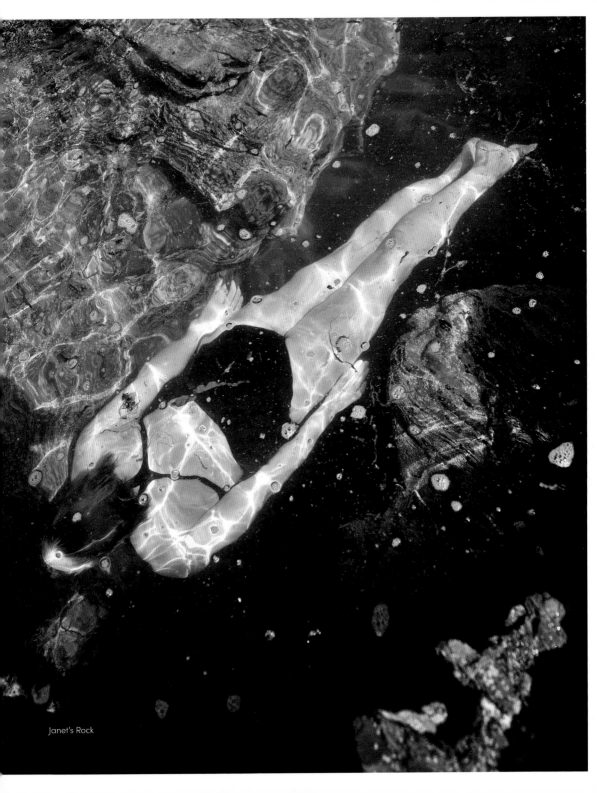

Janet's Rock

AT A GLANCE

44 JANET'S ROCK

Scramble over rocks and through small rock pools, then dive back into the sheltered bay to swim. From here, walk south along the strand towards Ballymartin where another path takes you back up alongside a small stream to the road. In nearby Kilkeel, check out Seascope NI beside the harbour, a lobster and marine hatchery which is open to the public.

BY CAR: 42 minutes from Newry. Take A2 to Warrenpoint and continue along the coast through Rostrevor and Kilkeel. Ballymartin is approximately 3 miles (5km) north-east of Kilkeel, heading towards Annalong. Janet's Rock is on the Annalong side of Ballymartin village.

Just beyond the village proper, a bus stop opposite several houses marks the laneway. Park in the lay-by and walk approx. fifty yards along the road to the lane down to shore.

BY BUS: Translink route no 37 runs between Newcastle and Kilkeel. Check their website for schedule.

FAMILY FRIENDLY • SECLUDED • ROCK POOLS • JUMPING WITH CARE

GRID REF: J 35155 17209
GOOGLE MAPS REF:
54.08556, –5.93558

45 BLOODY BRIDGE

Scramble up the river, exploring its waterfalls and pools. On the coast road from Newcastle to Annalong is the infamous Bloody Bridge. Named after a massacre during the 1641 Rebellion when the bodies are said to have been thrown over the bridge into the river, turning the water red with blood. This is also the start of the old smugglers' route, the Brandy Pad, once used to transport spices, brandy, wine, silk and tea from the Isle of Man through the mountains. It is now a popular walking trail. Squeeze through the narrow sheep gate and past the old bridge to walk up the path alongside the river. Approximately 10 minutes will bring you to the best of the deep pools where you can swim under the chilly waterfall or jump from the rocks into the steely cold waters fresh from the mountain.

BY CAR: 6 minutes from Newcastle. Take A2/Coast Road south past the harbour towards Annalong and Kilkeel for 3 miles (5km). The car park is on the left.

START OF HILL WALK • CAR PARK WITH TOILETS • FAMILY FRIENDLY • ROCK POOLS, SCRAMBLING • JUMPING

GRID REF: J389271
GOOGLE MAPS REF:
54.17500, –5.87302

46 BLUE LOUGH

After a hard day's hike take a cool dip in this beautiful pool nestled in the heart of the Annalong valley in the Mourne Mountains. Swim beneath the north tor of Slieve Binnian and the slabs of Slievelamagan. For a decent climb, take the route over Little Binnian and then scale Slieve Binnian's north tor to finally come down the steep path towards Blue Lough in the valley to the right with views to Ben Crom reservoir on your left. An easier route suitable for families is to walk from Carrick Little car park near Annalong, past the rocky outcrop of Percy Bysshe.

BY CAR: 25 minutes from Newcastle. Take A2 towards Annalong. At Glasdrumman turn right onto Quarter Road. The road turns sharply left after approx. 1.5 miles (2.4 km). Continue for another mile (2km) to the small car park on your right. Blue Lough is 2 miles (3.5km) along the well-worn track into the hills.

FAMILY-FRIENDLY HIKE AND SWIM • MOUNTAIN LOUGH • BEAUTIFUL VIEWS

GRID REF: J 32727 25186
GOOGLE MAPS REF:
54.15829, –5.96870

Blue Lough

(47) LOUGH SHANNAGH

Lough Shannagh, or Lake of the Fox, sits in the centre of the Mourne Mountains, above Ben Crom reservoir and beneath the steep slopes of Carn Mountain. This peaty, gently shelving mountain lough is perfect for cooling off on a hot day and is a favourite for half-day hikers, with two routes, one from south of the lough and one from the west. Two small beaches lie at either end, both north and south of the lough.

BY CAR: 16 minutes from Newcastle. Take Bryansford Road from Newcastle for 2.5 miles (4km), turn left onto B80 Hilltown Road, drive past the Tollymore Mountain Centre and then turn left onto Slievenaman Road for 3 miles (4.8km). Follow this road past Meelmore Lodge and Fofany Dam for 3 miles (5km). Ott car park is on the right.

Cross the road from the car park and climb over the stile. Follow the higher path at the fork and continue up to the wall, approx. 1 mile (2km). Climb the stile and continue down to the lough.

FAMILY-FRIENDLY HIKE AND SWIM • MOUNTAIN LOUGH • BEAUTIFUL VIEWS

GRID REF: J 27987 27855
GOOGLE MAPS REF:
54.18465, -6.04094

(48) ROSTREVOR

Sandwiched between the shores of Carlingford Lough and the steep slopes of Kilbroney forest, a gateway into the Mournes, Rostrevor is a must visit. Each summer, visitors from around the world enjoy a wealth of Irish music at the Fiddlers Green Festival.

The grass picnic area on the shore marks the original bathing area to the left. Steps lead down to a concrete plinth along the sea wall where ladders take you into the water. Best an hour either side of high tide. Add a stroll in Kilbroney Park with its Narnia experience for the kids or explore the Fairy Glen.

The sailing club has a small slipway with a gravel beach and parking for about seven cars. Be sure not to block the slipway.

BY CAR: 40 minutes from Newry. Take A2/Warrenpoint Road. As you approach the coast in Warrenpoint, turn left onto Queens Street/A2 and follow it for 2 miles (3km). At the roundabout, take the second exit onto Shore Road/A2. Approx. 0.5 mile (800m) brings you to the picnic area. Parking is on the roadside.

FAMILY FRIENDLY • JUMPING AND DIVING FROM JETTY

GRID REF: J 17983 17918
GOOGLE MAPS REF:
54.09697, -6.19688

㊾ DROMORE RIVER

COUNTIES CAVAN & MONAGHAN

Skip from Cavan into Monaghan and back again, as you front crawl or breaststroke along the Dromore River towards Drumlona Lough, weaving back and forth across the county border with each stroke as it cuts down the centre of the river. River swims close to towns are not something I usually recommend, but here in the heart of the lakelands the Dromore River is an absolute gem. Tall reeds line the riverbank as the swimmer quietly meanders along.

Cootehill has its fair share of the 365 loughs of Cavan, nestled between the rivers Dromore and Annalee. With 26 lakes within a 10-mile (16km) radius, ranging from the large Lough Sillan in the south to the small but beautiful Annaghmakerrig in the north, it is little wonder this area has been a favourite haunt for artists, writers, poets and playwrights, including Percy French and Seamus Heaney.

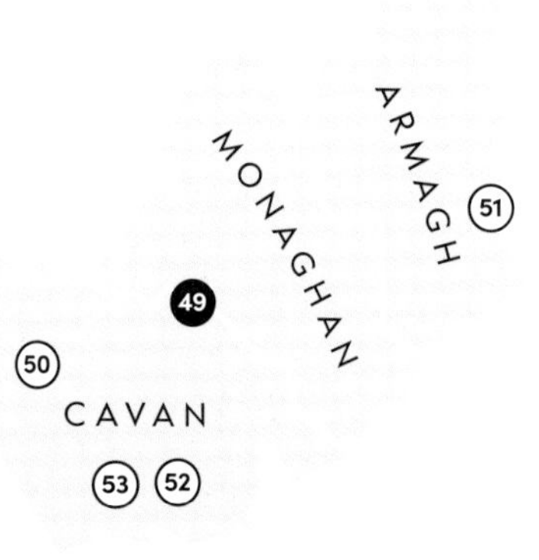

Along the shores of the river, teenagers lounge in small boats at the water's edge, so deep in conversation they hardly notice as you breaststroke by.

From Cootehill town centre, take the road out of town towards Dartry. Approaching the border between Cavan and Monaghan, you will cross an old bridge. Look for the small car park on the right and park there. Either swim from the grassy bank in shallow waters at the bridge or walk a little distance along the wooded pathway. Every so often a wooden boardwalk, only two planks wide, juts out from the path to a little jetty. Anglers use these stands and there is the occasional small boat tucked into the tall reeds. The opposite bank leads into Bellamont Forest, a 1,000-acre estate with woodlands and the first Palladian villa built in Ireland, Bellamont House, built by the Coote family.

Swimming is actively encouraged around Cootehill and few will bat an eye at a swimmer. During the summer water-safety classes are run here.

Have a quick dip or venture as far along the river as you wish. The flow is gentle and not too fast. If in any doubt of your swimming strength, first swim upstream to have the benefit of the flow on the return journey. This is always a good way to get a feel for how strong the flow is and may help you decide how far you are willing to swim each time.

Dromore River

AT A GLANCE

49 DROMORE RIVER

Enjoy a meandering river swim, passing small fishing stands and skipping from one county to the other along this border waterway. Popular with swimmers during the summer and running water-safety lessons for children, there is still solitude to be found by venturing farther downriver where the fishing jetties provide perfect access for the swimmer (just remember which stand you left your gear at).

BY CAR: 25 minutes from Monaghan town. Take the R188 towards Cootehill, continue for 23.5km. Look out for Abbott industrial on your right, opposite is the entrance to parking.

BY BUS: Bus Éireann has services from both Cavan and Monaghan. Check their website for schedules.

RIVER SWIMMING, EITHER DIP OR JOURNEY • LOCAL GROUPS • SCENIC WALKS NEARBY •

GRID REF: H 59741 15153
GOOGLE MAPS REF:
54.08225, -7.08722

Lough Oughter Castle

50 LOUGH OUGHTER

In the depths of Killykeen Forest Park, with its myriad walking trails and the lakes that form the southern Lough Erne complex, lies a tiny island, dominated by the Clough Oughter Castle ruins, a huge stone-built semicircle of wall that soars up towards the sky. The castle dates to the 13th century and is thought to have been built to protect the chieftains of the O'Reilly clan from warring neighbours. Then, in the 17th century, it was used as a prison. For the swimmer, it's a 300m swim across; stuff sandals and a towel into your dry bag to explore the castle ruins.

BY CAR: 30 minutes from Cavan town. Take N3 north, through Butler's Bridge. Turn left onto L1511 for 6km, continue onto L1508 for 2km, then turn left, signed Lough Oughter. After 1km reach the lakeside picnic area. From here you can swim to the island.

ISLAND SWIM WITH CASTLE • TOW-FLOATS AND SANDALS RECOMMENDED

GRID REF: H 35494 07709
GOOGLE MAPS REF:
54.01720, -7.45949

51 CAMLOUGH LAKE

A long-time favourite of swimmers and triathletes, this pretty lake sits below Slieve Gullion, close to Newry. The lake is sheltered, calm and has easy access from a wide slipway, providing an ideal training ground. In summer you will find something of a carnival atmosphere with children paddling, swimmers and triathletes enjoying the water. This is a place you are likely to be welcomed by many local swimmers.

Enter from the slipway on the Crossmaglen Road, where marker buoys form a variety of circuits from 250m to 750m. Newry Triathlon Club run events here through the year, including triathlons, courses and occasional night swims.

BY CAR: 28 minutes from Dundalk. Take the A1 north for 18km. Take the exit A25 Newry/Camlough/Downpatrick. At the roundabout take the first exit to Camlough.

Drive through the village and turn left onto B30/Newtown Road, signposted Silverbridge/Crossmaglen/Castleblaney. Continue for 800m to the lake and slip on your left. Parking along the lay-by.

POPULAR LAKE SWIM • DISTANCE MARKERS

GRID REF: J 02902 25920
GOOGLE MAPS REF:
54.17161, -6.42583

52 LOUGH RAMOR

There are 365 loughs in County Cavan, one for each day of the year. How to choose, then, where to swim? My advice is to check out Lough Ramor: it has camping on the lake shore, rowboats for hire and islands to swim out to and explore.

The swimming here is lovely, a gently shelving lake with 32 islands, some just a short swim from the campsite. Virginia is approximately 2.5km across the lough and if you want to swim the full length of the lough it is nearly 5km long. With no jet skis allowed, this is an ideal place for swimmers and kayakers. Check out Lough Ramor Camping if staying in the area.

BY CAR: 1 hour 10 minutes from Dublin. Head north west from Dublin on N3/Navan Rd for 70km. Turn left onto L3024/Munterconnaught for 3km, then turn right onto L3022/Lough Ramor. Continue for 5km and look out for the sign for Lough Ramor Camping on the right.

LAKESIDE CAMPING • ISLAND SWIMS • CONTACT LOUGH RAMOR CAMPING FOR ACCESS

GRID REF: N 57807 86029
GOOGLE MAPS REF:
53.82092, -7.12327

53 LOUGH SHEELIN

Lough Sheelin means 'the lake of the fairy pool' and with a name like that who could resist? This large lake crosses the borders of counties Westmeath, Meath and Cavan and, at 11km in length and 5km wide, it gives plenty of scope for the kayaker or swimmer. The swimming area near Crover is particularly well-placed, as you can go for an afternoon drink at Crover House Hotel and wander the lawns down to the water's edge to get spectacular views. The parking area leads to a grassy foreground and then a patch of coarse sand, laid each summer by the local council for swimming and life-saving classes. Beyond is a wide concrete slipway and, to the right, a long pier.

BY CAR: 25 minutes from Cavan town. Take N55 south for 14km. Turn left onto R154 for 5.5km, then right on to L7079, signed Crover House Hotel. Almost 1km to Crover Boat Quay.

FAMILY FRIENDLY • POPULAR LAKE SWIM

GRID REF: N 47119 86115
GOOGLE MAPS REF:
53.82303, -7.28502

Dunagree Point,
County Donegal

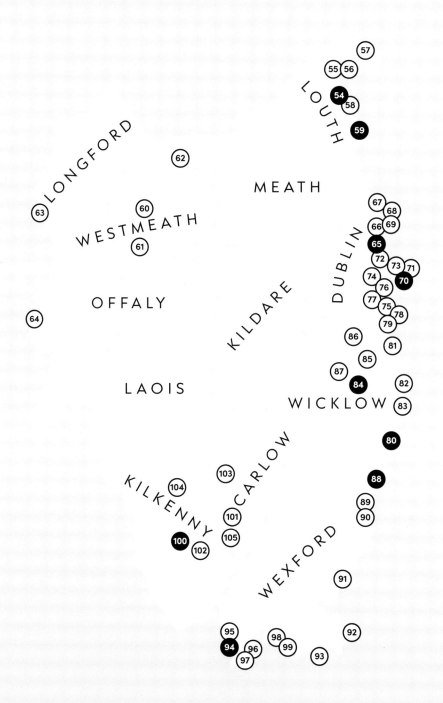

LEINSTER

THIS TOUR THROUGH THE PROVINCE will take you from the traditional city swims of Dublin and Dún Laoghaire, where you will meet with swimmers of all ages and perhaps follow in the footsteps of James Joyce, to Wexford's 'sunny south-east' with its long, golden strands. Take a dip in the peaty loughs of the Wicklow Mountains and then explore the quiet fishing piers in the loughs of the midlands. Enjoy the buzz and vibrancy at Lough Owel's diving board and finally, immerse yourself in the gently flowing rivers of Carlow and Kilkenny.

54 SALTERSTOWN PIER

COUNTY LOUTH

Salterstown Pier is the locals' gathering place to swim and picnic and while away lazy summer days. Those in the know say it is the best spot hereabouts. The low pier wall serves both as a windbreak and buffet table, laden with fruits and snacks to keep the revellers going. Swimsuits and towels lie stretched out to dry and the aroma of sausages wafts from barbecues across Dundalk Bay, with the backdrop of the Cooley Mountains across the bay and the Mournes hazy in the distance.

Whether the tide is in or out, the pier provides a perfect walkway into the clear water, free from the pebbles on the seabed. As barefoot children run back and forth, teenagers dive into the deeper water and search for crabs while other swimmers tour the length of the shore as far as they wish. The water is clear here and, although there is little beach to speak of, swimming from the pier creates a sense of adventure not to be found so easily at the nearby and popular beaches of Annagassan and Clogherhead.

After a full day's swimming, diving, exploring and admiring the views of the mountains, take the shore road north past Annagassan Beach and drive approximately 10km to the small town of Blackrock. With a lively seaside resort feel, it is a world away from Salterstown Pier. Stop at Café Acqua for an ice cream as the sun goes down and your body tingles with the memory of your swim.

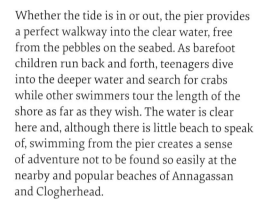

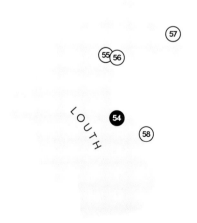

RIGHT Salterstown Pier

AT A GLANCE

54 SALTERSTOWN PIER

A long, narrow slipway reaching out into Dundalk Bay, the shore around it is stony and at low tide the sand is revealed.

BY CAR: 25 minutes from Dundalk. Take R132 south towards Castlebellingham, then R166 to Annagasssan. At the southern end of Annagasssan Beach turn left onto the scenic route along the shore towards Dunany Point. This quiet country road is perfect for a coastal cycle, past white stone cottages.

Alternatively, take M1 to Junction 15 at Castlebellingham, then R166 to Annagassan.

BY BUS: Bus Éireann runs a service from Dundalk to Annagassan. Salterstown Pier is on the Coast Road, almost 3.5km from Annagassan. Walk south east along the beachside R166 Strand Road, approx. 1.4km to a fork where the road sweeps to the right. Follow the left-hand fork onto Coast Road for 1.8km to reach Salterstown Pier.

FAMILY FRIENDLY • GOOD ACCESS FOR KAYAKS

GRID REF: O 11794 93347
GOOGLE MAPS REF:
53.87768, -6.30069

55 PRIESTS BEACH

Both Priests and Ladies' beaches sit at the northern end of Blackrock. Priests Beach is the larger of the two and popular with local swimmers who meet in small groups to enjoy a swim and a chat, taking the time for coffee and cake afterwards. The sand is fine and white, the water shallow and the beach feels intimate, protected from road noise by the mature trees of the garden above. With no parking at the beach, some park in town and walk the prom, others cycle and chain their bikes up at the small grass area where a ramp on one side and steps on the other lead down to the sand.

BY CAR: 11 minutes from Dundalk. Take R172 towards N52. At the roundabout take the second exit to stay on R172. At the next roundabout, take the third exit to stay on R172. Continue to the coast, passing Sandymount Beach and then Ladies and Priests Beach. Park in town and walk back. Both beaches are close to the church: look for the brown signposts for each.

POPULAR • FAMILY FRIENDLY • WALK FROM TOWN • CAFÉ AND SHOPS NEARBY

GRID REF: J 07434 03027
GOOGLE MAPS REF:
53.96552, -6.36359

56 LADIES' BEACH

A blue plaque tells us that the tall stone wall was built in the 1850s 'to afford the ladies privacy when they went to bathe'. The wall continues down to the rocks on the far shore, making this as cosy a cove as a beach in Ireland can be! A small patch of sand between jagged rocks and the seclusion can make you feel far from the bustle of the seaside town, the perfect place for a peaceful swim and quiet contemplation, and yet it's just a gentle walking distance when you're ready to return to the world.

Blackrock is a busy little seaside town with plenty of cafés and boutique shops along the front, buzzing with people of all ages enjoying the sunshine or a cuppa along the promenade.

BY CAR: 11 minutes from Dundalk. See directions for Priests Beach (above).

FAMILY FRIENDLY • SECLUDED • CAFÉ AND SHOPS NEARBY

GRID REF: J 07484 03108
GOOGLE MAPS REF:
53.96635, -6.36275

57 CARLINGFORD HARBOUR

For many years there has been a pier-to-pier swim on Christmas Eve in Carlingford Harbour, under the imposing King John's Castle, with soup served afterwards for the deserving swimmers.

There is easy access from either the slipway inside the harbour beside the sailing club or from the gravel beach outside the harbour wall. This historic village has plenty to offer for a weekend getaway. The narrow streets date back to medieval times and now house many pubs and restaurants, where you can't fail to get a good meal. Check out the 12th-century castle, cycle the 7km Carlingford Greenway to Omeath or join the Leprechaun Hunt on the mountain on the Sunday the clocks change in March.

BY CAR: 30 minutes from Dundalk. Take N52 north for 4km then exit onto R173. Passing Ballymascanlon Hotel, travel 18km towards Greenore. Turn left onto R176 into Carlingford. After 2.5km, turn right onto Ghan Road and follow the shore. Turn right into the sailing club. Limited parking.

POPULAR • FAMILY FRIENDLY • JUMPING AND DIVING • EASY ACCESS

GRID REF: J 19251 11826
GOOGLE MAPS REF:
54.04249, -6.17965

58 LURGANBOY/PORT BEACH

The wide strand of Lurganboy is a popular family summer day out, but with such a huge beach, you can always find a quiet spot. With views of the Mourne Mountains, it's great for a long beach walk and swim, yet not far from Dundalk town. The brightly painted lifeguard hut stands out on the dune and farther along the beach, wooden groynes lean into the sand, framing the Cooley Mountains across the water. The beach here shelves gently and is relatively protected, yet as always, in windy conditions any beach can get rough, so swim within your own capabilities. This is a super area to cycle, off-season. In autumn, the coast road is relatively quiet and the shoreline teems with migratory birds and there are plenty of places to stop to refuel.

BY CAR: 28 minutes from Dundalk. Take R132 to Castlebellingham, turn left onto R166 towards Togher and then left onto Togher Road for 2.5km. Turn right onto L2244/Coast Road to the beach car park.

POPULAR • FAMILY FRIENDLY • LONG STRAND

GRID REF: O 14512 87789
GOOGLE MAPS REF:
53.83211, -6.25881

Lurganboy/Port Beach

Ladies' Beach

59 CLOGHERHEAD AND PORT ORIEL

COUNTY LOUTH

With countryside to rival any on the west coast of Ireland, Clogherhead has a popular beach. Chalets line the rise behind the strand, making the most of their sea view. The gently shelving beach gradually fills as families come out to enjoy the sun, with all, including the family dog, racing into the waves before heading back up the beach for breakfast.

Taking the path from the beach, there is a pleasant walk from the village along the sea cliffs into picturesque Port Oriel Harbour. 'Be guided by the dancing starfish,' the locals say, referring to the metal sculpture on the harbour wall, welcoming visitors to the port.

This grassy track passes up over the headland, full of places to scramble and explore. Craggy inlets topped with mauve clover and white daisies lead down into deep gorges. Climb down one of these gorges to plunge in and, as you swim around the rock face, discover what remains of Red Man's Cave, almost inaccessible now after decades of marine erosion.

There are several gory tales as to how this place got its name: one set during the Cromwellian wars of 1649 tells of Cromwell's soldiers putting a number of Catholic priests to death here. Until recently, the cave was painted red to commemorate this event, but now time and the ravages of the sea have worn it away almost completely.

Another story tells of a Spanish ship's crew, many of whom had died of scurvy during their voyage to these shores. The remaining six and their captain camped at the cave but each night another man would die, until only three crew and the captain were left. Suspecting their captain of foul play, these last few men cut off his head and placed it in the cave. Legend says that, at night, a spectral man can be seen walking around the area, singing and whistling.

Moving back into the bright sunlight washes away the shivers of ghost stories. Follow the rocky coastline farther and soon come to the harbour.

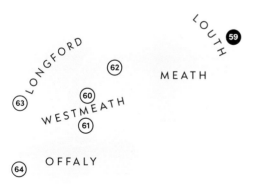

ABOVE Clogherhead
LEFT Lough Owel

AT A GLANCE

59 CLOGHERHEAD AND PORT ORIEL

Swim at the sandy beach or explore the rocks around the headland to Port Oriel. Look for the remains of Red Man's Cave and perhaps even hear the ghost as he whistles and sings. Call in at Fisherman's Catch for fresh seafood which has travelled all of 50m from the boat to the fishmongers' shelves.

BY CAR: 30 minutes south of Dundalk on the M1. Exit at Junction 12 onto R170 to Clogherhead and park at the beach. Alternatively, park at the harbour at Port Oriel, climb over the stile to the right of the harbour walk and starfish, and take the grassy track around the headland.

SCENIC WALK • LIFEGUARD DURING SUMMER • POPULAR • FAMILY FRIENDLY

GRID REF: O 16446 83569
GOOGLE MAPS REF:
53.78822, -6.23495

60 LOUGH OWEL

Lough Owel's diving boards are a star attraction. The parking area sits high above the lough, affording great views out towards Church Island with plenty of room to picnic. The path runs down to cross the narrow bridge spanning the railway line where, in summer, the steep grass banks are alive with youths and families soaking up the sun. Steep steps down to a long jetty lead out to the boards.

Concrete benches on the shore provide seating for those cheering encouragement to the divers. The water is clear and shallow close to shore but quickly gets deep enough for jumping and diving.

Lough Owel is also protected as a Ramsar site, a wetland of international importance due to its rare plants, variety of fish and migratory birds.

BY CAR: 8 minutes from Mullingar. Take N4/Sligo Road. Approx. 6km along this road, you will see the Lough Owel viewpoint car park on the left. Park here.

DIVING BOARDS • FAMILY FRIENDLY • PICNICS

GRID REF: N 41950 58559
GOOGLE MAPS REF:
53.57551, -7.36725

61 LOUGH ENNELL

The designated bathing waters of Lough Ennell make this a great spot for families. Close to Lilliput adventure centre and boat hire, there's plenty of scope for water sports. A large octagonal sandpit faces the slipway entrance to the bathing area. The jetty runs out into shallow water past a great bank of reeds. A concrete step runs the length of this jetty and at the far end curves around for easy access to and egress from the water. Large marker buoys show the designated swim area, which forms a wide triangle. No jet skis are allowed on the lake. Water Safety Ireland run summer courses here, yet all year round one can take a dip.

BY CAR: 1 hour 30 minutes from Dublin. Take N4 towards Lucan, onto M4 Galway/Sligo. Then take M6 Galway/Athlone. Exit at Junction 4 onto N52 towards Mullingar. Turn left onto L122 for Ballinagore, then right and follow signs for Jonathan Swift Park/Lilliput. Turn right at the adventure centre and right again to the car park near the shore.

FAMILY FRIENDLY • TOO SHALLOW FOR JUMPING OR DIVING

GRID REF: N 37739 44234
GOOGLE MAPS REF:
53.44694, -7.43306

62 LOUGH LENE

A jewel in Westmeath, Lough Lene has long been a family swimming haunt with clear waters and a pride in having been the first freshwater lake in Ireland to win the coveted Blue Flag award.
In the 1950s, a diving board was built out where the wooden jetty now ends and the tradition of swimming lessons that began in those days continues with Water Safety Ireland running courses each summer. Well used by fishermen, kayakers, SUPers and swimmers, this is a beautiful spot in the heart of the country.

BY CAR: 1 hour 30 minutes from Dublin. Take N3/Navan Road onto M3. Exit onto N3, then left onto R163. Travel 15.5km, turn left and continue 4km to Lough Lene parking.

FAMILY FRIENDLY • POPULAR • SUMMER SWIM LESSONS

GRID REF: N 53315 68135
GOOGLE MAPS REF:
53.66034, -7.19428

63 BARLEY HARBOUR

In the centre of Ireland sits the ancient Lough Ree and the dividing line between Leinster and Connacht runs down its length.
On its north-east shores in County Longford, the beautiful old-style stone jetty of Barley Harbour looks out to Inchcleraun Island, 2.5km across the tranquil waters. It was not always so tranquil. It was here on Inchcleraun Island that Queen Maeve returned for rest after the Táin wars and the death of Cuchulainn. However, a son of the King of Ulster followed her. When she came to bathe in the cool waters, he fired a slingshot, striking and killing her outright.

BY CAR: 2 hours 25 minutes from Dublin. Take M4 to Mullingar. At Junction 15, take N52/Mullingar. At the third roundabout, take the second exit onto R400. Continue onto R394 then R392 to Ballymahon. From there, continue on R392 for 8km then turn left and follow this road 10km to Barley Harbour.

SECLUDED LAKE SWIM • DIVING WITH CARE • ISLAND VIEW

GRID REF: N 01602 57583
GOOGLE MAPS REF:
53.56861, -7.97672

64 BANAGHER OUTDOOR POOL

On the banks of the River Shannon, Banagher Park holds a unique pool. A rectangle of pontoons creates an enclosed swimming pool, deep enough for jumping and with ladders for easy egress, it's a lovely spot to relax in the Shannon waters without worrying about the river's flow. This community-owned pool is free (at time of writing). Follow your swim with a picnic and explore Cromwell's Castle nearby.

Plans are for a rebuild of the pool including access ramps.

Technically, this pool sits in Galway as the border between Offaly and Galway runs through the River Shannon; however, Banagher is in Offaly.

BY CAR: 1 hour 50 minutes from Dublin. Take N4 to M4 Sligo/Galway for 60km. Continue onto M6 Galway/Athlone for 50km. At Junction 7, take R446 Moate, then turn left onto R444 for 10km. Turn left onto N62 and travel 14km. At Cloghan continue onto R356/Banagher Street. At Banagher, turn right onto Main Street. Cross the bridge and turn left for the pool.

FAMILY FRIENDLY

GRID REF: N 00430 15878
GOOGLE MAPS REF:
53.19357, -7.99426

⑥⑤ DONABATE

COUNTY DUBLIN

Paddle through the shallows, the water lapping around your ankles as you pick up and examine tiny shells, sand crunching beneath your toes, sandals swinging loosely in hand: such simple pleasure! This could have been any exotic beach, anywhere in the world, save for the sight that greeted us: fiery red hair above freckled skin, bikini-clad and wielding a hurley, she looked like a modern-day Irish Boudicca.

One could not have scripted such an encounter. This quiet beach was the perfect place to hone her skills. Running and laughing, she and her teammate passed the sliotar between them, trying to keep control of a steady volley back and forth, the gentle crack of ash on leather echoing across the strand. Only in Ireland, eh? But here's the rub: neither of the players was Irish. They were, in fact, French!

A public golf course backs onto Donabate and it is through here that a pleasant walk across the fairway on an old green road, still easy to make out as a low-lying grass track, leads onto the long strand. Dotted along the beach, there will be little family groups; parents watching children running in and out of the waves, bright picnic blankets a splash of colour against the pale sand. The huge strand runs for miles between the Rogerstown Estuary to the north and Broadmeadow to the south, both of which are designated Special Areas of Conservation and are superb locations for birdwatching. There is plenty of room here to get well away from the crowds and, at only 19km from Dublin city, it is very easy to get to.

Nearby Newbridge Demesne is a public park on 370 acres of 18th-century parkland, with woods, lawns and wildflower meadows. The mansion, Newbridge House, featured in the 1965 film *The Spy Who Came in from the Cold,* starring Richard Burton.

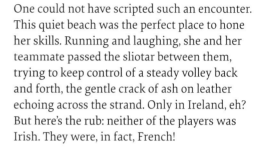

DUBLIN

RIGHT Donabate Beach

AT A GLANCE

65 DONABATE

A long and popular strand, Donabate is lifeguarded during the summer months. A café and hotel are nearby. Walk farther south along the beach beside the golf course for less busy areas. Donabate is 19km north-east of Dublin, and is served by both train and bus routes from the city.

BY CAR: 10 minutes from M1, exit at Junction 4, signposted for Donabate. Take R126 past Newbridge Demesne to Donabate town centre, then turn right onto New Road, heading towards the golf club. There is parking either beside the Waterside House, which is a popular stretch of the beach, or take another right turn and park on the road beside the golf links. A public right of way is signed to the beach.

POPULAR • FAMILY FRIENDLY • LIFEGUARDED IN SUMMER

GRID REF: O 25442 49444
GOOGLE MAPS REF:
53.47733, -6.11806

66 TOWER BAY BEACH

One not to be missed! The view from the clifftop car parking down into this cove at Portrane is stunning, with its stone boathouse, Martello tower and views across to Lambay Island 4km to the east. The Martello tower is a private residence. The beach shelves quickly into deep water affording the strong swimmer some great exploring along the cliffs to the right of the bay. If you are lucky, you may spot seals close by. For walkers, the coastal path takes you from Donabate to Tower Bay, 2km each way.

BY CAR: 36 minutes from Dublin. Heading north on M1, exit at Junction 4 and take R132/Skerries/Rush/Donabate. Continue on R132. At the roundabout, take the second exit onto R126. Follow this for 8.8km to Tower Bay.

BY BUS: routes 33D and 534 serve Donabate and Portrane (correct at time of writing; check Dublin Bus website for schedules.)

STEEPLY SHELVING • CLIFF EXPLORATION FOR STRONG SWIMMERS ONLY • COASTAL WALK

GRID REF: O 26228 50453
GOOGLE MAPS REF:
53.48940, -6.09718

67 SKERRIES

With two long beaches and stepped bathing spots, Skerries has plenty of choices for swimmers. The North Beach is generally more sheltered, so it's good for families. South Strand can be popular with windsurfers and kitesurfers but right in the middle, the Captains and Springers are man-made bathing areas where you can get into the water without touching the sand. The Springers, being closer to South Strand, can have strong currents, so it is for experienced swimmers only. Both are a short walk from Red Island car park.

BY CAR: approx. 46 minutes from Dublin. Heading north on M1, exit at Junction 4. Take R132 and then R127 to Skerries. Take the Harbour Road and, as you pass the harbour, turn right to the car park.

BY BUS/TRAIN: routes 33 and 33A from Dublin city (check Dublin Bus website for times). Skerries train station is a 2km walk from Red Island car park.

CHOICE OF SWIM SPOTS • JUMPING AND DIVING • STRONG CURRENTS AT THE SPRINGERS • DEEP WATER

GRID REF: O 25742 61110
GOOGLE MAPS REF:
53.58576, -6.10207

Portrane

Loughshinny

(68) LOUGHSHINNY BEACH

This small fishing village boasts a pretty beach sheltered by the harbour wall and the natural curve of the coastline. Gently shelving, it's ideal for families and in summer is lifeguarded. South, on Drumanagh Head, stands a 19th-century Martello tower. Take a walk up to the tower and look for the door that you would need a ladder to reach! With limited car parking, it's wise to get here early on hot days.

BY CAR: 1 hour 30 from Dublin. Go north on M1. Exit at Junction 4 for R132 Skerries/Rush. Turn right onto R127 Dublin Road and stay on R127 toward Skerries. Turn right onto L1285 and continue 4km to Loughshinny Beach.

BY BUS: take bus 33 or 33A from Dublin city (check Dublin Bus website for times) and alight at Loughshinny Cross, stop 3787. Take the L1320 on the right (signed Loughshinny) and walk 1km to the shore.

FAMILY FRIENDLY • FISHING PIER AND BEACH

GRID REF: O 27181 56894
GOOGLE MAPS REF:
53.54698, -6.08126

(69) RUSH BEACHES AND HARBOUR

With two long strands, north and south of the town, the sheltered harbour beach and the added bonus of a large swimming platform behind the pier wall, Rush has everything to offer swimmers of all levels. The beaches are sandy and gently shelving, and popular year-round with local swimmers. Marker buoys have been set up for distance swimmers. Depending on wind direction, you should find one of the two strands more sheltered than the other. The swimming platform is tucked in on the south side of the harbour wall, built on the rocks that edge the coast. **Make sure the water is deep enough before jumping in.**

BY CAR: 50 minutes from Dublin. Take M1 north, exit at Junction 4 onto R132 Skerries/Rush. Turn right onto R127, at Dublin Road roundabout, take the third exit onto R127/Rathmore Road. At Remount roundabout, take the third exit onto R128/Station Road. Continue for 5km through Rush to the pier. Limited parking at the harbour beach.

CHOICE OF BEACH • JUMPING AND DIVING AT PIER

GRID REF: O 27444 54267
GOOGLE MAPS REF:
53.52288, -6.07865

⓻⓪ HOWTH

COUNTY DUBLIN

Only ten minutes north east of Dublin city centre (30 minutes on the DART), Howth is a haven for seafood lovers. Howth Market (open weekends) is beside the DART station and sells crafts, jewellery, antiques and organic foods. From the harbour, there are four walking-route options with coloured arrows to guide you. The cliff path affords spectacular views of Dublin Bay and Ireland's Eye.

On the first weekend of summer a festival vibe sweeps along the coastal path from Howth as hosts of teenagers in swimsuits and shorts flock alongside tourists and walkers. The pier in Howth is out of bounds – swimmers will be fined if they jump from it – so instead they have reclaimed an old diving haunt a short way along the craggy coastline.

Turn left off the trail and drop down a rough, beaten track, making your way to the remains of a vertiginous staircase, where a rope aids the traverse down to the rocks below and leads to the outcrop where the concrete plinths for old diving boards still remain. The water is deep and clear, a natural diving pit.

It is only when one stands level with the board that one can appreciate the height. The lower board is perhaps 5m above the sea, the higher plinth close to 10m. There's a lot of time on the way down from 10m to realise that you just might have made a mistake!

Watch as teenagers line up on the cliff on the other side of the diving pit to leap and then swim across to a small rock in the middle of the cove to rest in the sun, a *Great Gatsby*-like vision of the seemingly endless summer.

As their confidence grows, younger boys push themselves to more daring dives, somersaults, spurred on by the crowd and adrenaline. The girls soon join them, somewhat tentatively before a few begin to brave the higher rocks.

DUBLIN

ABOVE AND LEFT
Howth diving, cliff path

AT A GLANCE

70 HOWTH

On Howth Head, walk the various trails or explore the several hidden coves off the cliff path where one can jump and dive into deep, clear waters not far from the harbour and vibrant village. Take the cliff path from the DART station following the purple arrows to the promenade along the harbour. At the end of the prom, turn right onto Balscadden Road and climb to Kilrock car park, where you join the path. As the trail climbs higher, look for a narrow track down to the cove. Push through long grass and bracken until, at a sharp left turn, you can see the rocks and diving plinths below. Continue down to the staircase and to the rocks, where you can leave your clothes, before swimming just a few metres to the high rock with the diving board and plinths.

BY PUBLIC transport: take the DART to Howth or 31A bus from the city centre (check DART and Dublin Bus websites for schedules).

BY BOAT: from Dún Laoghaire, south Dublin, Dublin Bay Cruises sail to Howth (check their website for schedules).

JUMPING WITH CARE • SCENIC WALK • GOOD FOOD

GRID REF: O 29864 39032
GOOGLE MAPS REF:
53.38585, -6.04879

Balscadden Cove

71 BALSCADDEN COVE

It's worth a little extra effort to get to this secluded cove. Less of a climb than the diving plinth above but still one for the more adventurous. Walking up Balscadden Road from Howth Harbour and passing the steps down to Balscadden Beach, look for a small gate in the seaward wall, approx. 350m from the beach. Through this gate, a little track winds down the cliffside to the rugged cove. Clamber over the rocks to reach the cool deep waters in the shadow of the cliffs. You might want to bring a mask and snorkel before returning to the shallows and the sunlight to warm up. Certainly, the climb back up the track will warm you after your dip!

BY PUBLIC transport: take the DART to Howth or bus H3 route from the city centre (check DART and Dublin Bus websites for schedules).

SCENIC WALK • GOOD FOOD • POPULAR

GRID REF: O 29167 39029
GOOGLE MAPS REF:
53.38584, -6.05919

(72) VELVET STRAND

Enjoy 5km of soft white sand at Portmarnock north of Dublin with a view across to Lambay Island, Ireland's Eye and Howth Peninsula. Popular all year round for swimming, walking and cycling along the prom. At the north end of the beach the *Eccentric Orbit* statue commemorates the first Atlantic flight from east to west by the *Southern Cross* in 1930. With Blue Flag status in 2023, the beach is lifeguarded during the summer months and water quality is monitored.

BY CAR: 35 minutes from Dublin. Head north on M50. Exit at Junction 3 for R139/Malahide. Stay on R139 for 2.7km. Turn left onto R107/ Malahide Road and then right onto R123 Balgriffin Road. Turn left onto R124 Drumnigh Road and right onto Station Road. Finally, turn left onto R106/Strand Road. Parking at two car parks.

BY PUBLIC transport: bus routes 32B and 42 stop by the beach (check Dublin Bus website for schedules).

POPULAR • LIFEGUARDED IN SUMMER • FAMILY FRIENDLY • DISTANCE SWIMS

GRID REF: O 24722 44182
GOOGLE MAPS REF:
53.43388, -6.12474

(73) BURROW BEACH

This swathe of strand near Sutton gets its charming local name 'Hole-in-the-Wall Beach' from the narrow entrance just off Burrow Road that leads between the houses to the shore. Within view of Portmarnock, you can see the 1.2km stretch that links, at low water, to Claremont Beach at Howth. A popular spot for walking, swimming or simply lounging on the sand. With very limited parking close by, your best bet is to use public transport.

BY PUBLIC transport: 15 minutes from Sutton DART station. From Station Road, turn left onto Lauders Lane and then right onto Burrow Road. Approximately 700m along is the narrow entrance to the beach. (Check DART website for schedules.)

SCENIC WALK • FAMILY FRIENDLY • LIFEGUARDED IN SUMMER

GRID REF: O 26670 39684
GOOGLE MAPS REF:
53.39228, -6.09661

(74) BULL ISLAND

Bull Island on Dublin city's north side continues to grow towards the sea, with miles of sandy beach, dunes, mudflats, grasslands and marsh. The island became Ireland's first official bird sanctuary in the 1930s and in 1981 achieved UNESCO Biosphere Reserve status. Created 200 years ago, this sandspit was formed with the construction of the North Bull Wall. Swimmers gravitate to the steps along the sea wall where changing areas face the port and the great Poolbeg chimneys. Swim at mid to high tide (at low tide you will be walking back across the sand flats). Public toilets are beside the visitor centre and there is car parking on the beach.

BY PUBLIC transport: 20 minutes from the centre of Dublin, take the 130 bus route to Bull Island, stop 1752. Walk across the bridge to the island.

BY CAR or bicycle: take the Clontarf Road from Dublin city. The Wooden Bridge at Clontarf, close to the port, leads to the bathing area on the south-west end of Bull Island.

SCENIC WALK • CITY SWIMMING • FAMILY FRIENDLY

GRID REF: O 21423 35739
GOOGLE MAPS REF:
53.35403, -6.16758

⑦⑤ FORTY FOOT

COUNTY DUBLIN

The beauty of Dublin city swimming is its accessibility via public transport, with DART stations near each site. This conveys the impression of the city as a series of villages that have been amalgamated into the metropolis as it has grown, although each village has managed to keep its own identity. Dublin is a vibrant, living thing and at its heart a pulse of cyclists, runners, walkers and swimmers all keep it thriving.

The Martello tower above the rocky cove features in the opening scene of James Joyce's epic novel *Ulysses* and houses the James Joyce Museum.

For 250 years, Dubliners have been leaping into the sea here. Joyce himself was a keen participant, and in *Ulysses* refers to 'the sea, the snotgreen sea, the scrotumtightening sea'. This promontory on the southern tip of Dublin Bay was, until the 1970s, exclusively a gentlemen's bathing area and, because it was isolated and for men only, became popular with nudists. The nearby Sandycove Harbour was the ladies' and children's bathing area. Since women's rights activists plunged in from the 1970s, the Forty Foot has welcomed all. The sign remains, though: 'Gentlemen's Bathing Place'

There is a narrow entrance that opens out to a changing area. Painted walls block the worst of the offshore breeze and a small lip at the top provides a modicum of shelter on rainy days. Steps lead down into the water with a single handrail to help steady you on slippery rocks. At the bottom step, the only thing to do is launch yourself forward and out into this craggy bay.

Although many people dive in from the rocks, it is dangerous. Take heed of the warning signs and ensure you know the depth. Sandycove Bathers' Association help with the upkeep of the area, which is funded by voluntary donations. It is a short walk from the Forty Foot to Sandycove Harbour.

DUBLIN

The Forty Foot

AT A GLANCE

75 FORTY FOOT

The Forty Foot is popular with all ages and levels of swimmer and for anyone visiting Dublin, it really is a must-see place. A craggy cove with steps and ladders into the water, it has the added bonus of the sheltered Sandycove just a short walk away.

BY PUBLIC transport: take the DART to Sandycove/Glasthule. Turn right, heading south on Glasthule Road. Take the first left onto Islington Avenue towards the shore, then turn right and walk 10 to 15 minutes along the front. You will see the tiny Sandycove Harbour at the end of the bay. From the harbour, there is a narrow path to the Forty Foot and the Martello tower.

BY CAR: 14 minutes from M50 junction 16. Take the R118/Dún Laoghaire for 4km. At Graduate roundabout take the third exit onto L3027/Killiney. Continue to the end of this road, turn right onto R119, after 200m turn left signed James Joyce Tower. Follow the road past Sandycove where it sweeps right. In 200m turn left onto the cul de sac. Limited parking along the shore.

JUMPING WITH CARE • CITY SWIMMING • EASY ACCESS

GRID REF: O 25829 28210
GOOGLE MAPS REF:
53.28955, −6.11369

Great South Wall

76 GREAT SOUTH WALL

Accessed through the docks, the Great South Wall reaches out into the centre of Dublin Bay. Halfway along this lengthy jetty, you will find the Half Moon Swimming and Water Polo Club. The whitewashed building provides shelter for swimmers enjoying the fabulous views back towards the port dominated by the Poolbeg chimneys.

BY CAR: 30 minutes from M50 junction 6, exit onto N3/Navan Road. Keep right to stay on Navan Road for7km. Continue onto R101/ North Circular Road, 2km. Turn left onto Sheriff Street, passing Dockyards Station, continue for 1km. Turn right onto R131/East Wall. At the roundabout, take the second exit onto Tom Clarke Bridge/R131. At the roundabout, take the second exit. After approximately 200m, turn left and continue through the docks for 1.3km.Turn right (restricted height road) and follow on to Shelly Banks car park and Great South Wall parking.

ON FOOT: about 1 hour's walk from the city centre or take the Red Line of the Luas tram service to Point Village. From here, walk through the Docklands and alongside the beach to Great South Wall.

SCENIC WALK • GOOD FOOD AND PUBS • SHALLOW BAY • CITY SWIMMING • ICONIC VIEWS AND SWIM

GRID REF: GREAT SOUTH WALL: O 22359 33860
GOOGLE MAPS REF:
53.34116, −6.16388

(77) SEAPOINT BATHING AREA

A long rocky strand with steps and slipways making for easy access. It's best at high tide and you will find swimmers here year round. Standing at the north end of the beach, the Martello tower is now the headquarters of the Genealogical Society of Ireland. Changing areas are tucked around its base and, below this, a wide bank of steps leads into the water. The beach is a Special Protection Area (SPA) for birdlife and has won Blue Flag status for several years. Seapoint monitors water quality and will issue no-swim notices if it drops. Submerged rocks at the south end of the beach call for caution when swimming at low water.

Lifeguarded during the summer months, this can be a busy spot and popular with all ages.

BY DART: alight at Salthill and Monkstown station. Cross the bridge over the lines to the prom, the Martello Tower to your left, and walk for 10 minutes. (Check DART website for schedules.)

POPULAR • FAMILY FRIENDLY • LIFEGUARDED DURING SUMMER • SWIMMING AND WATER SPORTS

GRID REF: O 22727 29062
GOOGLE MAPS REF:
53.29749, -6.15919

(78) THE VICO

One of the last bastions of 'au naturel' swimming, the Vico is quieter and harder to find than the Forty Foot but well worth the effort. Swimwear is optional.

Climb from Dalkey along the Vico Road and take the path noted below. As it zigzags down the steep hillside with fantastic views of Dalkey Island on the left and Killiney Bay to the right, you get your first view of the Vico bathing area. To one side a small, sheltered seawater pool mirrors the sky.

BY CAR: 3 minutes from Killiney. Take the Victoria and then Vico Road past Victoria Park. At White Rocks Bathing Area, there is a lay-by with car parking space. Walk from here as there is no parking farther along. As the road sweeps left and drops down, look for a small gap in the wall on the seaward side. Take this path, across the footbridge and down to the Vico bathing area.

NATURIST AND SKINNY-DIPPING • CITY SWIMMING • ROCKS AND ROCK POOL

GRID REF: O 26943 25950
GOOGLE MAPS REF:
53.26919, -6.09702

(79) KILLINEY BEACH

Just a little farther south from the Vico, you can find the sweeping, stony strand of Killiney, a very popular beach with views south to Bray Head. Year-round swimmers can be found here enjoying this Blue Flag beach. With good access for all users, it can be busy, so get here early in the summer months! Gently shelving, it's a great place for family swimming and, for those who fancy a walk, there are several routes nearby up Killiney Hill to fantastic views across the bay and out to the Wicklow hills.

BY CAR: from Dublin, take N11 south to Killiney and follow the signs to the car park near the DART station (paid parking). Walk from here under the road and rail tracks to the beach.

BY DART: alight at Killiney. (Check DART website for schedules.) From the station turn right and walk 50m towards car park entrance. An underpass gives access to the beach.

POPULAR • FAMILY FRIENDLY • LIFEGUARDED DURING THE SUMMER

GRID REF: O 25995 24655
GOOGLE MAPS REF:
53.25751, -6.11252

⑧⓪ SALLYMOUNT NATURIST BEACH

COUNTY WICKLOW

Less than an hour's drive south from Dublin, Brittas is one of the best-known beaches in Ireland, a 5km stretch of sand and dunes along the Wicklow coast. While the main beach is very popular with families and has several camping and caravan sites, farther south is the little-known naturist beach: Sallymount.

Swimming nude feels great: no suit to chafe the skin, the whole body feels the water and, when getting out, no struggling out of a soaking swimsuit while trying to preserve modesty under a flapping towel. The naturist simply strides out of the water and lets the air and sun do the drying: much more comfortable!

WICKLOW

The tide is turning in favour of 'au naturel' swimming and there are now growing numbers of people who strip off for charity; the 'Dip in the Nip' in aid of cancer charities encourages hundreds of people to jump naked into the sea,.

Although there are many secluded beaches around Ireland that naturists use, there are, in fact, no officially approved naturist beaches. Public nudity is still somewhat taboo in Ireland but attitudes are beginning to thaw, and the Irish Naturist Association, which has been in existence for over fifty years, continues to campaign for official clothing-optional facilities.

In the 17th century, the infamous pirate Captain Jack White operated from the cove now known as Jack's Hole, smuggling goods from British merchant ships and importing from France, avoiding customs. He had a lucrative business until his accomplice, the sheriff of the Grand Jury, felt that Jack was getting too bold and had him tried and hanged.

Brittas is a popular family beach and many come here to walk and swim. The water gets deep gradually and at the height of summer the beach can be busy. Walk south of the main beach to find the naturist area where you can swim and sunbathe at ease.

RIGHT Sallymount
Naturist Beach

AT A GLANCE

(80) SALLYMOUNT NATURIST BEACH

The naturist area is a long, sandy beach at the southern end of the main beach.

BY CAR: 30 minutes from M50/ N11 junction south of Dublin. Continue for 42 km, exit at junction 19, R773/Brittas Bay. At the roundabout take the third exit R772, and continue for 3km. At the roundabout, take the first exit onto L6177, then turn left to stay on L6177 for 800m. Turn right onto Sandymount (signed Brittas Bay). At the end of this road turn right and park on roadside, the small gate to the sand dunes path is opposite. It is a 15-minute walk through dunes.

As there are no officially approved naturist beaches in Ireland, swimming or sunbathing nude on a public beach is illegal. The website of the Irish Naturist Association recommends using discretion and common sense to avoid problems and says that no member of the association has yet been prosecuted for naturist activities.

NATURIST AND SKINNY-DIPPING • SAND AND DUNES

GRID REF: T 28887 79721
GOOGLE MAPS REF:
52.85350, -6.08501

(81) GREYSTONES

Greystones is a very popular summer and weekend destination with two long beaches, one on either side of the harbour, and the small Cove beach, which has become extremely popular. The North Beach is stony, hence the name Greystones, and so the sandy South Beach and the Cove are the busier areas. It shelves quickly to deep water, so **caution should be taken with children and less confident swimmers**. Only a 50-minute drive from Dublin and serviced by a regular DART service, it can get very busy during the summer.

BY CAR: 50 minutes from Dublin. Take the M50 south. Continue onto M11 and then N11. Take R762 exit toward Delgany. At the roundabout, take the first exit onto R762/Glen Road. At the next roundabout, take the first exit onto R762/Mill Road. Follow Mill Road to South Beach car park.

POPULAR • SHELVES QUICKLY

GRID REF: O 29641 12656
GOOGLE MAPS REF:
53.14879, -6.06267

(82) TRAVELAHAWK BEACH

With such a name, who could resist visiting this beach! Only a stone's throw from Wicklow harbour with a climb down a steep set of steps you find yourself cocooned under the remains of the Black Castle in this stony cove. With steeply shelving waters it's best for strong swimmers but if the conditions are fine you might venture around the cliffs to view seals in their favoured spots.

Walkers might check out the Wicklow Town Heritage Trail, a 4km looped walk, which starts at Glen Beach south of the town and affords great sea views.

BY CAR: 1 hour 35 minutes from Dublin. From the M50, take the M11 south. Exit onto R772. At the roundabout, take the first exit onto R750/Main Street. Continue to Castle Field. Limited parking at the end of Castle Field joining Castle Street. From here, a concrete footpath leads towards the Black Castle and shore. Steep steps down to Travelahawk Beach below.

STEEPLY SHELVING • STONY BEACH • EXPERIENCED SWIMMERS ONLY

GRID REF: T 32273 93968
GOOGLE MAPS REF:
52.98045, -6.03089

Magheramore Beach

(83) MAGHERAMORE BEACH

Walk for 750m along a pretty lane under the canopy of trees to get your first glimpse of this beautiful white-sand beach. A world away from the bustle of Wicklow town, you can shake off the day's worries as you plunge into the Irish Sea. If you come here off season, you may well have the whole place to yourself. There are rock pools to explore at either end and yet the main strand is clear and affords a smooth, uninterrupted swim from north to south, almost 400m, the perfect training ground for doing laps.

BY CAR: 13 minutes from Wicklow town. Take R750 for 7km to Magheramore. Turn left down to the beach. Limited street parking or park in the field, €5 for the day (at time of writing)

FAMILY FRIENDLY • WALK TO BEACH

GRID REF: T 32985 88477
GOOGLE MAPS REF:
52.93047, -6.02317

⟨84⟩ GLENDALOUGH

COUNTY WICKLOW

South of Dublin and nestled in the Wicklow Mountains National Park, Glendalough has long been a tourist attraction. With its ancient monastic settlement, two loughs and trails ranging from easy to strenuous, families can while away a full day here.

Early morning, as the mist rises from the water, you are treated to a vista of the lough. In autumn, as the leaves begin to change colour on the trees lining the slopes on both sides of the glen, you might imagine yourself in New England or Canada.

WICKLOW

An important site of Irish Christian heritage, Glendalough's ancient churches, round tower, and the famous St Kevin's Cross continue to attract visitors year round. Born into a noble family of Leinster in AD 498, Kevin was called towards the spiritual from a young age. Moved to live simply while studying the Christian faith, he settled at Glendalough, the perfect place to live as a hermit, close to nature. One legend tells of a blackbird laying an egg in his outstretched hand as he prayed. So in harmony with nature and animals, it is said he remained there until the egg hatched.

Another, darker story tells of an ancient monster that once lived in the Upper Lake. As the monastic city grew and more people settled here to study under Kevin's tutelage, the creature would prey on the congregation. They moved to hunt and kill the monster, but Saint Kevin could not condone this. Instead, he entreated the creature to move to the Lower Lake. No recent attacks have been reported!

As you walk along the boardwalk to the petite Lower Lake you might catch glimpses of deer in the long grass meadows.

Get there early, as Glendalough is a very popular tourist site, and walk some way around the lake-shore path to find a quiet spot to swim. Glendalough regularly hosts a large swim event alongside walking, running and triathlon events, so check their website for when to visit.

ABOVE AND LEFT
Glendalough
Upper Lake

AT A GLANCE

84 GLENDALOUGH

While away a day in these idyllic surroundings.

BY CAR: 1 hour 15 minutes from Dublin. Take the M50 south. Exit at Junction 15 onto the road for Cornelscourt/Kiltiernan. At the roundabout, take the third exit onto Glenamuck Road N. At Kiltiernan, turn left onto R117/Enniskerry Road. At Enniskerry, turn right onto R760 to Ballybawn. Turn right onto R55 and continue past Vartry Reservoir. Continue on to Glendalough. There are large car parks and toilet facilities.

POPULAR • FAMILY FRIENDLY • ANCIENT MONASTIC SITE • WALKS

GRID REF: T 12399 96976
GOOGLE MAPS REF: 53.01234, −6.32988

85 LOUGH DAN

A walk with incredible views of the Wicklow hills, the chance to see herds of deer roaming the hillsides and a cool swim in the black, peaty waters. Coursing through the blackness, tiny golden bubbles rise from the disturbed silky water.

A bit of a hike, it takes the best part of an hour down to Lough Dan – and it's a good warmer on the way back up! No need for hiking boots. At the lakeside there are some sandy areas making for easy access to the water and it gently shelves.

BY CAR: 1 hour from Dublin. Take the M50 south onto M11 and then N11. Exit onto R755 towards Roundwood. At Vartry Reservoir, turn right onto R759. Continue for 3km where there is limited parking on the roadside near Luggala Lodge. Access is to the side of the large metal gates. Close to Ballinastoe Woods and boardwalk.

WALK TO LAKE • SECLUDED • SCENIC

GRID REF: O 17251 06460
GOOGLE MAPS REF: 53.09617, −6.25082

86 LOUGH BRAY UPPER AND LOWER

Tucked into the hills lie the two Bray loughs. Typical mountain loughs with rocks and fresh peaty water, it can be a bit of a clamber in but that's all part of the fun! Swim shoes or sandals make it much easier and you'll want walking shoes or boots for the trek in and out. Park in the little lay-by tucked under the slopes of Powerscourt Mountain. The narrow trail on the opposite side of the road leads down to the Lough Bray Upper. For an easier walk, Lough Bray Lower is a little farther down this road. The path across the bog to the lough can be slippery so good shoes are called for and you may find yourself pushing through the undergrowth to choose an entry point.

BY CAR: 55 minutes from Dublin. Take the M50 south. Exit at Junction 12 onto R113/Firhouse. Turn right onto Scholarstown Road, continue onto R113. Turn left onto L4003/Kilakee and continue for 2km. Turn right onto R115/Old Military Road for 10.5km, passing the Lower Lough to the Upper Lough trail. Park in the little lay-by.

SECLUDED LAKE SWIM • WALKING BOOTS AND SWIM SHOES NEEDED • SCENIC

GRID REF: O 14250 15138
GOOGLE MAPS REF: 53.17476, −6.29203

(87) LOUGH OULER

Ireland's heart-shaped lake is an hour's hike to get to but worth the effort. As with most mountain lakes, the water is dark and deliciously cold! A good level of fitness is required for this beauty but the reward for the steep climb is one of the most photo-worthy lakes in the county. Although a popular walking area, the path can be elusive, especially in winter. From the Glenmacnass waterfall car park, walk up the road (north-west) to the small forest on the left. A track here leads down to the river: cross this and follow the track on the right-hand side of the stream uphill to the lake. An OS Discovery Series 56 map is needed for this. Check the weather before attempting this and remember that in fog or mist one can easily lose one's way.

BY CAR: 1 hour 30 minutes from Dublin. Take R115/Military Road to the Sally Gap. Stay on R115 until you come to the car park at Glenmacnass waterfall. Walk from here as described above.

EXPERIENCED WALKERS • MAP SKILLS NEEDED • MOUNTAIN LOUGH

GRID REF: O 11349 03037
GOOGLE MAPS REF:
53.06647, -6.33926

Lough Ouler

Lough Dan

❽❽ KILMICHAEL POINT

COUNTY WEXFORD

Kilmichael Point is just south of the Wicklow/Wexford border, a mere 6.5km from Arklow and the popular Clogga Strand. From Kilmichael Point, there is a series of tiny sandy beaches just perfect to clamber down to and find your own private swimming cove. You can also walk a grass track along the dunes south, all the way to the sweeping strand of Castletown Beach.

Following the signs from Arklow for Kilmichael Point brings you finally down a narrow lane to a dead end with a small turning circle and a pretty terrace of stone cottages. This row of now-refurbished homes was originally built as a coastguard station in the mid-1800s. There are several small sandy coves here, each bordered by a flank of rocks, to which you can scramble down from the front of the terrace. The water is shallow and it is nice to swim at low tide or paddle around the rocks from one bay into the next. Spend a quiet afternoon here enjoying the small coves that stretch both north and south of Kilmichael Point.

On the other side of the row of cottages, a rough grass track goes south along the coast through the Kilpatrick sand dunes. The remains of several buildings are dotted across the fields, perhaps farm dwellings long abandoned. A small, square building, now deserted, seems to have been a lookout sometime in the past with a wide opening facing the sea. As you head south towards Castletown, each rise leads to a new cove, enticing you to explore farther. After fifteen or twenty minutes' walking, you come to a great swathe of sand sweeping across the grass into the centre of the fields – odd, like a desert in the middle of an oasis. It looks as if the beach is invading the fields behind. Now you have reached Kilpatrick beach. From this approach, you will find a quiet corner. Kilpatrick is known for its interesting and rare seashells.

Kilmichael Point

AT A GLANCE

88 KILMICHAEL POINT

A series of small sandy coves that can be climbed down to, or take a walk along the coast path south to the sand dunes of the popular Kilpatrick and Castletown beaches. A small turning circle provides some parking space in front of pretty stone cottages, originally a coastguard station, built *c.*1847 and now residential.

BY CAR: 1 hour 20 minutes from Dublin. Take M11 past Bray and Wicklow town to Arklow. Exit at Junction 21 and follow R772 from Arklow and Clogga towards Castletown. Before reaching Castletown, turn left, signposted for Kilmichael Point, which leads to a terrace of three stone cottages. Limited parking at cul-de-sac.

SECLUDED • FAMILY FRIENDLY • SCENIC WALK

GRID REF: T 25509 66598
GOOGLE MAPS REF:
52.73626, -6.14344

89 BALLYMONEY BEACH

Ballymoney offers two beaches, each with both Blue Flag and Green Coast awards. They are clean, popular family beaches. As they are used year round by local swimmers, it is best to get there early, or visit in spring and autumn as summer gets very busy. Parking at Sea Road brings you to the south beach, and a track leads from here over the low headland to the larger Ballymoney Bay Beach, which is lifeguarded during the summer. Walk north along the beach where several rock outcrops hide further sandy bays all the way to Kildermot Beach. These are not lifeguarded and you will need to watch the tide to ensure you are not cut off, leading to a scramble over the headland!

BY CAR: 1 hour 30 minutes from Dublin. Take the M50 onto M11 south through Arklow. At Junction 22, exit onto R772/Gorey. At the roundabout, take the third exit; at the next roundabout, take the first exit to stay on R772/Arklow. After 2km, turn right and continue for 5km to Ballymoney Beach.

FAMILY FRIENDLY • LIFEGUARDED DURING SUMMER • POPULAR

GRID REF: T 21584 60106
GOOGLE MAPS REF:
52.67866, -6.20294

90 KILTENNELL BAY BEACH

This beach has a little something apart from Wexford's rolling strands. Gently shelving with golden sand, it is perfect for families. For a longer swim, stroke out towards Kiltennell beach 1km north. The bonus of the trail from Courtown Beach, leading through the unusual wooded dune system of Courtown Dunes and Glen, with stunted sycamores growing on the peaks of sand dunes, this is a site of ecological importance. The trail leads through the dunes, past Kiltennell Bay Beach and on to Kiltennell Beach proper. Keep a lookout for wildlife; herons, woodpeckers, kingfishers and seals are abundant in the area. Check out the Seal Ireland Visitor Centre for information and tours.

BY CAR: 10 minutes from Gorey. Take R742 to Courtown. Head for North Pier, turning left onto Burrow Road. Park at Courtown Beach car park and walk northwards along the trail for approx. 800m to the beach. Alternatively, carry on along Burrow Road to the small car park at Kiltennell Bay Beach (where there are height restrictions).

FAMILY FRIENDLY • WOODED DUNES • WILDLIFE

GRID REF: T 20357 57356
GOOGLE MAPS REF:
52.65440, -6.22157

91 BALLINESKER

Between Cahore Point and the tantalisingly named The Raven is a series of immense strands of the 'sunny south east' – a ribbon of beaches running one into the next. Even on the warmest of days, you are bound to find some space to yourself. Ballinesker, a Blue Flag beach close to the Wexford Wildlife Reserve, is famous for its starring role in Steven Spielberg's *Saving Private Ryan*. The beach was the scene for the Allied landing in 1944 at Omaha, Normandy. Tom Hanks trod the sand here and the pub was even renamed the Omaha Café during the shoot.

Lifeguarded during the summer, this east-facing beach can kick up some surf, so **caution** should be used on windy days.

A side trip to Raven Wood for forest walks is a must.

BY CAR: 30 minutes from Enniscorthy. Take R744 to Blackwater. Turn right onto R742. After approx. 5km, turn left to Ballinesker Beach car park. A short sandy path leads over the dune to the beach.

POPULAR • FAMILY FRIENDLY • LIFEGUARDED IN SUMMER • CAR PARK

GRID REF: T 11719 28814
GOOGLE MAPS REF:
52.39986, -6.35925

92 SAINT HELEN'S BAY BEACH

South of Rosslare, Saint Helen's Bay Beach at the southern end of Burrow Bay Beach offers a beautiful swim. To the left of the small pier, a track leads past a row of houses and down onto the beach. Make your way through the rocks to fine golden sand. Explore the rocks at low water or walk the expansive stretch of sand towards Burrow. This is a great spot for families to while away the day. From late August, you may get the chance to gather a few blackberries along the track.

BY CAR: 15 minutes from Rosslare. Take N25 heading inland. Turn left onto Ballyknockan and continue to Ballyaddragh. Turn right onto Riscrann and then on to Ballywitch. After a sharp left-hand bend in the road, take the first right down to the pier. (The golf club is straight ahead at this turn.) Parking at the pier.

FAMILY FRIENDLY • SWIMMING

GRID REF: T 14511 09857
GOOGLE MAPS REF:
52.22886, -6.32435

93 KILMORE QUAY

A local meeting point, the busy Little Beach is nestled beside the harbour wall and is a stone's throw from all Kilmore's cafés, an art studio, a chipper and the popular harbour itself. It gets deep quickly.

The long spit of St Patrick's Bridge can be seen at low water curving south from the shore almost 1km to the left. The story goes that St Patrick chased the Devil out of Ireland. As he reached Wexford's coast, St Patrick had gained on him and hurled rocks, chasing him out to sea – finally forming this rock bridge!

The Kilmore Quay 4.5km looped walking trail makes its way from the harbour and through a memorial garden dedicated to those who lost their lives at sea and on towards the Ballyteige Burrow Beach. Alternatively, take the 20-minute boat trip out to the Saltee Islands bird sanctuary.

BY CAR: 28 minutes from Wexford. Take the R730 south to N25/Rosslare, 6.5km. Turn right onto R739/Kilmore Quay. Continue 16km to Kilmore Quay Harbour. The little beach is to the left of the harbour, parking at the harbour.

FAMILY FRIENDLY • VERY POPULAR • WALKS • CAFÉ

GRID REF: S 96664 03334
GOOGLE MAPS REF:
52.17361, -6.58755

⓰ DOLLAR BAY

COUNTY WEXFORD

Close to the border of Wexford and Waterford is the long finger of Hook Peninsula, said to have been the origin of the saying 'by hook or by crook' in 1170 by Robert Fitz Gilbert de Clare, Earl of Pembroke. On his way to capture Waterford, he reputedly instructed his men to land at either Hook, on the Wexford side of Waterford Estuary, or by the village of Crooke in Waterford. At the very tip, Hook Head is Ireland's oldest working lighthouse. If you don't want to tour the interior, simply enjoy the grounds and the sea views.

The Ring of Hook coastal drive takes you past crumbling ruins and the Templar Inn restaurant, famed for its seafood, to many small beaches. Approximately 8km north of Hook Lighthouse, Dollar Bay is signposted as a sea-fishing beach. Quiet, with high, sandy cliffs that curve around to several rocky outcrops and give shelter from the prevailing winds, this secluded beach is good for swimming at either high or low tide.

Dollar Bay was named for the hoard of Spanish milled gold that was buried here by mutineers in November 1765. The brutal tale tells of how four crewmen of the *Earl of Sandwich* attacked and killed their shipmates and captain, all save the cabin boy. They flooded the ship and watched it capsize, ignoring the poor cabin boy's cries as he scrambled up the mast. The robbers rowed away with 250 sacks of gold, almost two tonnes, coming ashore at Dollar Bay. Only able to carry one bag of gold between them, they buried the rest of the sacks in the sand. As they made their getaway towards Dublin, the sinking ship drifted to shore at Sheep Island with the cabin boy still clinging to the wreck. Rescued, he told his story and the search began for the mutineers. News of four men spending Spanish gold spread quickly and they were soon caught and hanged for their crimes.

No need to rush here with a shovel, though: all the gold was recovered and the beach is now a place where you can swim in tranquillity, with no trace of the underhand dealings of the past.

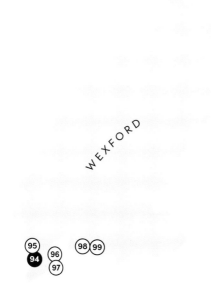

ABOVE Dollar Bay
LEFT Cullenstown
beach

AT A GLANCE

94 DOLLAR BAY

A sheltered, sandy beach, which shelves gently to beautiful swimming in a shallow cove.

BY CAR: 45 minutes from Wexford. Take N25 towards Rosslare. Turn right onto R733 through Wellingtonbridge and on towards Arthurstown. Turn left onto R734 towards Fethard-on-Sea and the Ring of Hook coastal drive, passing the Templar Inn. After a few kilometres there is a left turn signed for Dollar Bay Beach Fishing. Park along the lane and walk the steep gravel path down to the beach.

FAMILY FRIENDLY • SECLUDED • GOOD FOOD • BEACH CAMPING • SHRIMPING AND SNORKELLING

GRID REF: S 75068 05570
GOOGLE MAPS REF:
52.19726, -6.90154

95 BOOLEY BAY

Booley is a gem of a beach with golden sands and several Green Coast awards. It has the benefit of a large, flat grassy area, perfect for wild camping above the high-water mark. High sandy cliffs curve around the beach with several rocky outcrops providing shelter from the prevailing winds. Great for shrimping, the best being at low tide in the rock pools to the right of the beach. If seafood is your thing, check out the nearby Templar Inn.

BY CAR: 20 minutes from Wellingtonbridge. Head west on R733. After 10km, turn left onto R737 for 2km, then left onto L4045 for 2.8km. Turn right at the fork and continue towards the shore. Roadside parking so can be busy on peak days.

POPULAR FAMILY BEACH • KITESURFING • SHRIMPING

GRID REF: S 75009 06020
GOOGLE MAPS REF:
52.20147, -6.90371

96 BAGINBUN BEACH

It is hard to resist visiting a place with the hobbit-esque name of Baginbun. This tranquil bay holds a dark history, however. It had been a military stronghold since 500 BC, and in 1170 Raymond le Gros led a band of around eighty men in the second Anglo-Norman invasion, choosing Baginbun as a defence camp before attacking Waterford. Raymond's men brought back a herd of cattle after a raid. At this, between 1,000 and 3,000 Waterford men marched on Baginbun, confident of beating the small army. Raymond, however, ordered his troops to attack and then retreat in feigned panic. As the Waterford men charged after them, Raymond loosed the cattle in a stampede, scattering his attackers, killing many and capturing more.

BY CAR: 20 minutes from Wellingtonbridge. Head west on R733 towards R736. After 8.3km, turn left onto R734. Continue for 8.5km through Fethard and then turn left to follow the track to shore. Limited parking and a walk down to the beach.

POPULAR FAMILY BEACH • STEEP TRACK TO SHORE

GRID REF: S 80073 03392
GOOGLE MAPS REF:
52.17658, -6.83073

97 CARNIVAN BAY

Approximately 2km south of Fethard-on-Sea and 8km north east of Hook Head Lighthouse, this picturesque bay sits below Baginbun Head, with its distinctive Martello tower dating from the Napoleonic Wars. The steep sandy cliffs form a sun trap, and the path leads down to a fine golden strand popular with families, who come to picnic and play.

This long south-facing beach can be subject to waves and strong undercurrents, so it is for strong, experienced swimmers only. Good surfing and windsurfing. To get to the beach, there is a short walk along the top of the sand cliffs, then a steep path down.

BY CAR: 20 minutes from Wellingtonbridge. Head west on R733 towards Arthurstown, then R734 to Fethard and follow the signs to Baginbun Head. Park at the top of the cliffs and follow the rough track above the beach to the steep path down.

POPULAR FAMILY BEACH • STEEP PATH TO SHORE • STRONG SWIMMERS ONLY

GRID REF: S 79909 03169
GOOGLE MAPS REF:
52.17547, −6.83804

98 BLACKHALL BEACH

A small out-of-the-way beach in south Wexford, the rocky and sandy cove of Blackhall Beach has a sea arch to the right which, in calm conditions, you can swim under. The Keeragh Islands lie 1.5km off the coast, surrounded by a reef. There were several shipwrecks here and, in the 1800s, local people built a shelter on one island for the sailors. Now the ruins can be seen only from the air. Tucked away, this beach is perfect for an evening dip or paddle to watch the sun go down over Ballyteige Bay.

BY CAR: 35 minutes from Wexford. Take R733 to Wellingtonbridge. Turn left onto R736 for 4km. Turn left onto Grange Street. After 1.5km turn right and continue 1km down the narrow lane to the beach.

STRONG SWIMMERS ONLY • SEA ARCH

GRID REF: S 85173 07643
GOOGLE MAPS REF:
52.21385, −6.75434

99 CULLENSTOWN BEACH

The gorgeous Shell Cottage, dating back to the 1700s, overlooks the strand of Cullenstown Beach. Decorated with over 50,000 seashells it took over thirty years to achieve. The beach itself is sandy, gently shelving and south-facing so it's beautifully warm in summer, and it is one of the less busy beaches. There are views to the Hook Peninsula and Keeragh Islands which lie 1.5km out to sea. As a breeding ground for great cormorants, the islands are a Special Protection Area, so view from a distance. The Saltee Islands sit to the south east and, if you enjoy a sauna, the mobile Saltee Sauna pitches here too.

BY CAR: 35 minutes from Wexford. Take R733 for 14km, then turn left towards Duncormick. After 4.5km, turn left and then right. After 3.5km, turn right onto R736. After 1km, turn right and after 1km, turn right again and follow the road 1.5km down to the beach parking and Shell Cottage.

FAMILY FRIENDLY • PHOTO OPS

GRID REF: S 87659 07872
GOOGLE MAPS REF:
52.21604, −6.72126

ⓘⓞⓞ KINGS RIVER

COUNTY KILKENNY

The bridge across the Kings River in Kells has a charm all its own. This double-arched structure sits just upstream of Mullins Mill weir, forming the boundaries of a beautiful little swim spot. Shallow, with a stony floor, this is one for families. The flow during the summer is not too strong. Swim under the arches where ivy covers half the bridge wall, bindweed curls its way up one of the piers and in the central arch a bramble reaches down to the water surface.

The wide arches on the downstream side lead to narrow arches on the upstream side of the bridge. Along the weir, close to the bridge, a square is formed by the walls where the water boils and bubbles, giving a jacuzzi effect. Some folk like to sit in this cold outdoor spa!

The handsome if aged Mullins Mill overlooks the pool and houses the Kings Mill Restaurant, a craft centre run by Gwen, who also does millinery, and a museum (not open at time of writing). The surrounding gardens have signs up to say they are 'managed for wildlife' and as such create a tranquil setting.

From here you can follow a loop walk that takes you up the road, past pretty cottages with crocosmia and daisies leaning over the fence, and then back to the riverbank past a second redundant mill. This easy walk carries on a short distance to a bridge, crossing over to Kells Priory, founded in 1193. The three-acre site is worth a wander. Some local swimmers also pop into the water just downstream from the priory. From here it's a short walk back into the village.

If it has rained a lot prior to your visit, you may want to skip this walk – or bring your wellies for the muddy section! There may be cattle in the area and plenty of bird life.

RIGHT Kings River, Mullins Mill

AT A GLANCE

100 KINGS RIVER

Kings River was named after the local king, Niall Caille, drowned trying to save his servant who had fallen in. The servant survived, but Niall lost his life and the river was named in his honour. The river is also a Special Area of Conservation and homes the protected white crayfish, whose presence indicates good-quality water.

During the summer the local kayak club takes lessons at the mill.

BY CAR: 19 minutes from Kilkenny. Take N10 south onto N76. At the roundabout, take R697 exit. After approx. 10.5km turn left to park at Mullins Mill, just before crossing the bridge.

RIVER SWIM • RIVERSIDE WALK • PARKING

GRID REF: S 49484 43670
GOOGLE MAPS REF:
52.54237, -7.27132

Clashganny Lock

101 CLASHGANNY LOCK

Clashganny Lock is a very popular spot for swimmers, canoeists, kayakers and SUPers. On a hot day in summer, you may meet a wealth of folk laden with camping and picnic gear. Down at the lock, two lifeguarded swim areas provide ample space for swimmers. The first of the swim areas is here at the lock. However, turn right and walk upstream past the lock gates and you will find, by our reckoning, a far nicer swim area. The water cascading over the weir creates an infinity pool; and this boundary can be deep enough to dive from. (Be sure to check the depth for your own diving style!)

BY CAR: 35 minutes from Kilkenny. Take R712. Turn right onto R702. Continue on R702 through Gowran and Borris, then turn right just after the viaduct onto R729. Take the right turn signed Clashganny House Restaurant and follow the narrow road down to limited parking at the lock, which gets busy in the summer. Facilities include a large toilet block and the Little Black Box Coffee trailer for refreshments.

POPULAR • KAYAKING • LIFEGUARDED IN SUMMER • COFFEE TRAILER

GRID REF: S 73590 45991
GOOGLE MAPS REF:
52.56036, -6.91580

102 THOMASTOWN ISLAND WEIR SWIMMING AREA

Curved stone steps, which also serve as seats to perch on, provide easy access to this long, narrow pool. You can hear the rush of the weir while you swim in the mild flow. On summer afternoons there is a steady stream of locals and visitors. The old-world charm of the Grennan Mill Craft School with its multi-paned windows and mature gardens sets a calming scene.

Nearby, Happy Valley Coffee do a mean hot chocolate, sourcing their chocolate from the local chocolatier, The Truffle Fairy in town – another place well worth a visit!

BY CAR: 24 minutes from Kilkenny. Take N10 and then R700 at Bennetsbridge roundabout. At Thomastown, turn left onto Lady's Well Street. At the roundabout, take the third exit onto Maudlin Street. Turn right onto Low Street and then left onto Market Street R448, crossing the bridge and turning right. There is roadside parking opposite Grennan Mill Clothing. It's a pleasant walk along the lane to the Island Weir swimming area and Grennan Mill Craft School.

LIFEGUARDED IN SUMMER • FAMILY FRIENDLY

GRID REF: S 58309 41439
GOOGLE MAPS REF:
52.52146, -7.14157

(103) BAGENALSTOWN

It's three for one in Bagenalstown, where outdoor swimming is in the veins of the residents. Their **heated outdoor pool** is incredibly popular with booking open during summer months. On the River Barrow, **the Steps** is the traditional swimming spot right beside the outdoor pool. Wide concrete steps provide easy access into deep water and opposite, the long expanse of the weir wall provides a diving platform. The river's flow can be very strong so heed the lifeguard's advice. Downstream is **the Boatslip**. The river narrows here, so the flow gets even stronger, and the water rushes over another weir. **In rivers, always swim upstream first to test the strength of the flow.**

BY CAR: 25 minutes from Kilkenny. Take R712 to Paulstown and continue onto R448. Turn right onto R724 at Royal Oak stores. Stay on R724 through the town, turning left onto R705/724 at the Railway House. Turn right and then left following R705/ The Parade to the river. Turn right, passing the Boatslip. The outdoor pool is 1km farther along the riverbank, park here.

HEATED OUTDOOR POOL • RIVER SWIMMING FOR STRONG SWIMMERS

GRID REF: S 70705 62616
GOOGLE MAPS REF:
52.71073, -6.95462

(104) KILKENNY WEIR SWIMMING AREA

On Bleach Road to the north of Kilkenny city is this narrow swimming area, popular with locals who can travel here by bicycle. Shallow close to the wall and with not too strong a flow, it is perfect for families. The water gets a little deeper as you venture farther across the river. The depth is subject to change depending on water flow and past rainfall. The area is lifeguarded during the summer.

BY CAR: 11 minutes from Kilkenny Castle. Head north west on the Parade to Rose Inn Street. After 850m turn right onto Vicar Street. Turn left, staying on Vicar Street, then turn right to cross the river. Turn left onto Green's Hill and after 600m turn left onto Bleach Road. Follow for 1.5km, past Harrys Architectural Salvage, to the lay-by. The swimming area is behind the wall.

FAMILY FRIENDLY • CLOSE TO TOWN • LIFEGUARDED • LIMITED ROADSIDE PARKING.

GRID REF: S 50158 58434
GOOGLE MAPS REF:
52.67500, -7.25911

(105) GRAIGUENAMANAGH

A river swim close to town. You might meet canoeists hauling out after a long day's paddle, desperate to stretch their legs. The arched bridge which spans the river is lit up at night and, with riverboats moored along The Quay, the whole place has a lazy holiday feel. Along The Quay you'll find a broad set of steps in front of the rowing club and here many will take a jump **(be sure to check the depth when you visit)**. Just a short amble farther upstream onto the grass path is another swim spot with a minute sandy beach. It shelves gently here so you can walk into the peaty water.

BY CAR: 35 minutes from Kilkenny. Take R712 for 8.8km and then turn right onto R702 for 4.5km. Turn right onto R448 and after 2km turn left. After 3km, turn right and continue for 9km into Graiguenamanagh. Turn left onto The Quay before crossing the bridge.

BY BUS: 1 hour from Kilkenny Castle. Kilbride Coaches run a service at noon and 6 p.m. (at time of writing)

FAMILY FRIENDLY • RIVER SWIM • RIVERSIDE WALKS

GRID REF: S 71043 43705
GOOGLE MAPS REF:
52.54071, -6.95136

Clashganny Lock,
County Carlow

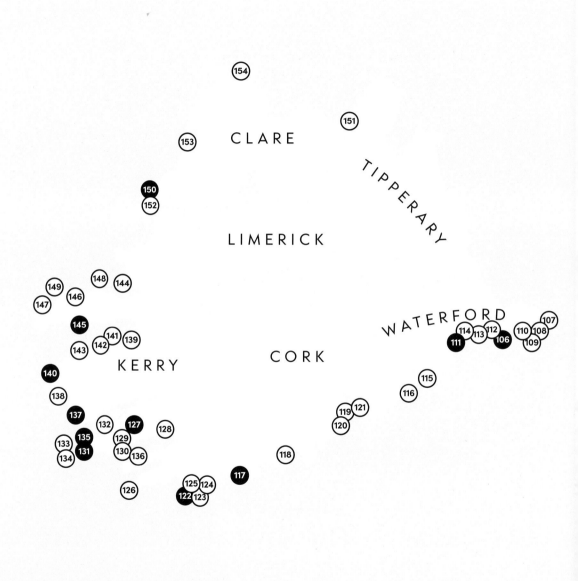

MUNSTER

THE KINGDOM OF MUSIC AND arts, Munster also has a wonderful range of outdoor swims, from popular spots to hidden gems. Dive from the boards at Guillamene on the Waterford coast and explore the craggy coves along the Copper Coast. Local favourite Goat Island is a treat not to miss as you journey farther west. Join distance swimmers at their training grounds at Sandycove Island near Kinsale, swim at beautiful Lough Hyne in Cork or Fenit Beach in Kerry. Enjoy incredible views on the Ring of Kerry and take a dip in the third-largest lake in Ireland, Lough Derg, with shores in three counties: Clare, Galway and Tipperary.

106 GUILLAMENE AND NEWTOWN COVES

COUNTY WATERFORD

Despite the 'men only' sign, all visitors are welcome at Guillamene and it is a must-swim at the gateway to the Copper Coast. The community of swimmers has grown here over seventy years or so and, while children and teens throw themselves from the diving board and casual swimmers enjoy the deep waters, adventure swimmers can explore a remarkable cave swim.

Just 3km from the busy promenade at Tramore, the coves of Newtown and Guillamene have been popular for swimming for over seventy years. As one follows the signs for the swimming club, the road sweeps down to a wooded area. A track leads into the trees from the roadside footpath: this is the entrance to the 'ladies' bathing area of Newtown Cove. Continue on to the ample car park at Guillamene.

The board at Guillamene is approximately 3 metres above the water (depending on the tide) and ladders to climb out are dotted around the cove.

Approximately 1km along the coast, there is a large cave. Deep and black and reverberating with the low boom of the moving water, it feels threatening to swim into but one can indeed swim right through and out the far side. It is an exposed and advanced swim from Guillamene to the cave and so suitable for strong swimmers only. From Guillamene Cove turn right and follow the coastline for approximately 1km. High on the cliff above is the statue of the Metal Man pointing out to sea. Watch out for the mouth of the cave between two outcrops of jagged rock. The opening is a tall, narrow arch leading into inky depths. Listen to the echoes as you stroke your way inside and your eyes adjust to the darkness. The water gets shallow as you clamber over the stones onto this subterranean shore. To the left, light seeps in through a low arch and here you can swim back out into the daylight world. You are now at the western end of Tramore Bay. To return to Guillamene , keep the shore on your left as you retrace your strokes, passing the large opening where you first entered the cave.

ABOVE AND LEFT
Newtown Cove
diving boards

AT A GLANCE

106 GUILLAMENE AND NEWTOWN COVES

The twin coves of Guillamene and Newtown are 3km from Tramore promenade, popular swimming holes with a thriving swim community. Swim the exposed kilometre along the coast to the large cave under the Metal Man.

The Newtown and Guillamene Swimming Club maintains the area and promotes it, ensuring the diving board and steps to access the water are kept clean and litter free.

BY CAR: 30 minutes from Waterford. Take N25 south west towards Dungarvan and Cork, then R682 to Tramore. From here, take the coast road west and follow signs for Newtown and Guillamene. Turn left to Newtown Caravan and Camping, and then left again to Newtown and Guillamene Swimming Club. There is a path through the woods down to Newtown Cove. Park on the roadside or continue around to the large car park at Guillamene where you can access either cove via steep steps.

FAMILY FRIENDLY • SWIMMING, JUMPING, DIVING • ADVENTURE SWIM • CAVE SWIM

GRID REF: X 57138 99404
GOOGLE MAPS REF:
52.14391, -7.16481

107 DUNMORE EAST

The 'sunny south-east' of Waterford lives up to its holiday reputation with pretty villages, great pubs and super coves to swim. This lively little town seems to run down the hill straight to the slipway where holidaymakers and locals enjoy a bowl of fresh mussels after their swim at Lawlors Beach.

In evening sunshine, you may find the port bustling, a live band playing music on the balcony of the Strand Inn, while outside the bar, swimmers mingle with customers. Beers are on the tables, towels laid out on the low wall nearby. The steep slipway into the water is directly below the Strand Inn. A second, popular beach is Councillors Strand with plenty of parking and a steep path zig zags down to the beach.

BY CAR: 25 minutes from Waterford. Follow R683 north east past the hospital towards Passage East. Passing the turn for Passage East, continue on R684 to Dunmore East. Approaching the shore and slip turn left onto Granville Terrace then right onto Crab Cottage, follow round to beach parking above Councillors Strand.

FAMILY FRIENDLY • GOOD FOOD • SCENIC WALK

GRID REF: S 68850 00795
GOOGLE MAPS REF:
52.15481, -6.99427

108 PORTALLY COVE

The rough, stony beach at Portally Cove is a secluded, sheltered spot, the perfect place to enjoy the evening sunshine. The high rocky walls gleam golden as they catch the last rays of the sun. The road down to the cove is extremely narrow so the best way to get here is to walk the 2km cliff path from Dunmore East. As always with a cliff walk, do not attempt this in high winds. From the public car park on the shore side of Dunmore East Harbour, walk along The Flatrocks, parallel to Convent Road. The walk starts at the end of this row of houses.

Alternatively, walk or cycle from Dunmore East Harbour. Take Convent Road and then turn left and continue for 1.4km. Turn left, signed Portally Cove. Go down this narrow laneway. At the last cottage, a narrow footpath leads down to the cove.

BY CAR: 30 minutes from Waterford. Take R683, then R684, to Dunmore East. Park at the public car park on the west side of the town, at Harbour Village. Walk from here.

SCENIC WALK • FAMILY FRIENDLY

GRID REF: X 67397 99065
GOOGLE MAPS REF:
52.13984, -7.01623

(109) RATHMOYLAN COVE

Another of Waterford's little gems hidden along its craggy coastline. Continuing west from Dunmore East, you will find some super deep inlets with small sandy beaches nicely sheltered from the open sea. The cliff path from Dunmore East takes in Portally Cove, above, and goes onto Rathmoylan Cove and is a beautiful way to enjoy unrivalled views of this rugged coast. Overlooking the cove, The Nissen Hut provides a swimmer's ideal holiday accommodation – book early if you fancy this spot all to yourself to enjoy the early morning vista across the bay. There is no parking at Rathmoylan so it's a walk or cycle from Dunmore East. On foot, take the cliff path for 4.5km from the public car park at Harbour Village at the west of the town. There is a downloadable map on visitwaterford.com.

BY BICYCLE: 16 minutes from Dunmore East. Travel west along the South East Coastal Drive for 4km. Turn left at the sign for cycle route 1. It is 0.5km down to the shore.

SHELTERED SWIM • 4.5KM
CLIFF PATH WALK • NO
PARKING • NO FACILITIES

GRID REF: X 65682 98846
GOOGLE MAPS REF:
52.13798, -7.04111

Ballymacaw Cove

(110) BALLYMACAW COVE

Scattered all along the Waterford coastline are sheltered coves and swimmers are spoilt for choice! Ballymacaw is sheltered on both sides by rocky promontories and the small stony beach shelves gradually. Follow the path on the left of the cove to make your way across a little bridge to the landing platform about halfway out along the headland: perfect for jumping at high water.

As with Portally Cove, above, it is possible to take the coastal walk all the way from Dunmore East to Ballymacaw. A good 7km one way, it's a challenging walk requiring a good level of fitness. This is an exposed coastal walk with steps and undulations. Be sure to check weather and wind conditions beforehand.

BY CAR: 10 minutes from Dunmore East. Drive west out of Dunmore East past Beach Cove Holiday Homes. Continue past the caravan park. After 5km on this road turn left onto Coastguard Station, leading down to Ballymacaw Cove. Limited roadside parking.

FAMILY FRIENDLY • JUMPING
AND DIVING • COASTAL WALK

GRID REF: X 64656 99041
GOOGLE MAPS REF:
52.13976, -7.05584

⑪ BALLYDOWANE

COUNTY WATERFORD

With jagged rocks and promontories that shelter each bay from the next, the best way to explore the Copper Coast is by car or bicycle. This rugged coastline has 25km of scalloped beaches and bays, named after the 19th-century copper mines that have helped to form the many sea arches and caves. Pretty villages and thatched cottages line the route of the South-East Coastal Drive, passing one cove after another.

This is a series of sand and gravel beaches, the cliffs ranging in colour from grey through red to purple, and pockmarked with the trademark holes and caves. Despite the rough and sometimes brutal landscape, the water is warm and many of the coves shelve gently, providing lovely swimming.

At Ballydowane, between Bunmahon and Stradbally, the entrance to the beach is not inspiring: a narrow laneway leads to a basic parking circle which then peters out into a short ramp onto the beach. Two great stacks on either side of this ramp hide the true expanse of the bay. It is only when you step out from their shadow that the view opens out and your breath is taken away by the rugged landscape. With fine grey sand, dotted with bright yellow and white seashells, stepping onto this beach is like entering another world. The cliffs hold inside them a primeval scene, and huge sea stacks jut out of the water like mythical sea creatures. Here the rocks are home to a wealth of fish if you want to try and catch your supper, or simply enjoy some interesting snorkelling in the shallow water. **The deep waters are suitable only for strong swimmers** due to the tides and currents here. Always swim parallel to shore and within your depth unless you have an accompanying kayak.

While swimming across the bay, look up at the great walls enclosing the beach. The layers of crumbling rock have been marked by each winter storm, changing the shape of the cliffs as they are battered by wind and waves.

RIGHT Ballydowane

AT A GLANCE

⑪ BALLYDOWANE

The sandy beach of Ballydowane Bay is surrounded by impressive red-brown cliffs and has rock pools to explore, good swimming across the bay and snorkelling around the sea stacks. The water gradually gets deeper. There are some currents here which make it **suitable only for strong swimmers**. To the far left of the bay, the prominent shark-fin-shaped stack is fun to investigate. Swim around it and see if you can find the narrow entrance to the cave underneath.

BY CAR: 25 minutes from Dungarvan. Take R675 towards Tramore. Follow this road and take the right-hand turn for Stradbally. In Stradbally, take the right-hand turn signposted for Ballyvoony. After a few kilometres, take another right turn, this time signposted for Ballydowane Bay.

STRONG SWIMMERS • ROCK POOLS • SNORKELLING • LIMITED ROADSIDE PARKING

GRID REF: X 40765 97906
GOOGLE MAPS REF:
52.13186, -7.40509

⑫ GARRARUS BEACH

The narrow entrance onto Garrarus Beach opens up when you walk down the steps into a view that wouldn't look out of place in a film such as *Journey to the Centre of the Earth*. With jagged rocks at either end of the bay and outcrops several hundred metres out, it cries out for some prehistoric creatures**! It is liable to strong waves so be sure the conditions are right for you.** Here you can camp on the grey sand beach, practise some bodysurfing, snorkel or maybe even catch a fish for your supper.

BY CAR: 9 minutes from Tramore. Head south west on Gallwey's Hill. Turn left onto Newtown Road. At the roundabout, take the second exit onto Newtown Hill. Turn left onto Newtown Park, continuing onto Newtown Glen, passing the caravan park. Continue 2km then turn left, from where it is 1km down to beach.

STRONG SWIMMERS • SNORKELLING • BEACH CAMPING

GRID REF: X 54705 98419
GOOGLE MAPS REF:
52.13551, -7.20212

⑬ KILFARRASY BEACH

Signed for Kilfarrasy Beach Fishing, this is a longer beach than its neighbour, **Garrarus**. The same rocky extensions reach out on either side of the bay and a large island sits about 400m out, with caves to explore. At the right (west) end of the beach, past the rocks, the second headland is crowned with a sea arch. On the left (east), one can scramble around the rocks to another bay which is quieter and more secluded.

Kilfarrasy can be popular so head around to the second bay to escape any crowds – but **be mindful not to get cut off, as the tide comes right in** to the rocks at high water.

BY CAR: 13 minutes from Tramore. Head south west on Gallwey's Hill. Turn left onto Newtown Road. At the roundabout, take the second exit onto Newtown Hill. Turn left onto Newtown Park, continuing onto Newtown Glen, passing the caravan park. Continue for 4.4km and then turn left to Kilfarrasy. Or take R675 west, turn left at Fenor towards Kilfarrasy, which is 2.5km away.

FAMILY FRIENDLY • POTENTIAL TO GET AWAY FROM CROWDS • POPULAR • CAVES

GRID REF: X 52635 98277
GOOGLE MAPS REF:
52.13443, -7.23269

(114) TRÁ NA MBÓ

A beautifully hidden beach with a tall narrow stack, like a totem pole standing tall in the gravel beach, at low tide completely abandoned by the water. Holes and caverns created by mining in years past now provide homes to wildlife: rabbits, hares, foxes and birds. Park in the small car park behind the lifeguard hut at the busy Bunmahon Beach, and walk up the stone road passing several houses, then onto a rough track. After five minutes' walk, take the narrow trail on the left. At the fork, take the right-hand path to weave your way down the steep slope to Trá na mBó.

BY CAR: 30 minutes from Tramore. Take R675, which goes all the way to Bunmahon. The small car park is straight ahead as the road bends right just before Bunmahon village and the main beach car park. Follow the path on foot up away from the beach and over the headland.

STRONG SWIMMERS • SECLUDED

GRID REF: X 42756 98196
GOOGLE MAPS REF:
52.13429, -7.37619

(115) GOAT ISLAND

The pretty Goat Island, 5km from Ardmore village, is secluded and tricky to find, but the reward is a picture-perfect little beach with golden sand, sheltered by rocks on either side, and with a great sea stack.

It is a nice, undulating drive or cycle up, past the round tower and out along country roads to the small car parking area above this little cove. The track that drops down to the sandy beach is narrow and steep. The beach is south facing and, although mostly sheltered, **during strong winds, there can be quite a surf.**

BY CAR: 25 minutes from Dungarvan. Take N25 towards Youghal. Turn left onto R673 to Ardmore village. At the staggered crossroads in the centre of the village, turn slight right and then left to drive up Tower Hill towards the church and round tower. Turn right at the tower and follow the road to a sign pointing left to Goat Island. Follow this lane down to a small parking area above the beach.

FAMILY FRIENDLY • SECLUDED • BEACH CAMPING • SURF IN STRONG WINDS

GRID REF: X 16531 77027
GOOGLE MAPS REF:
51.94545, -7.76125

(116) KNOCKADOON PIER

This little harbour packs a punch, with a handy slipway into crystal-clear waters, views of Capel Island and a coastal path with 2.5km and 6km loop walks. Enjoy swimming in the shelter of the harbour beach, the only spot for entering the water on this rocky coastline.

Warm up with a brisk walk along part of the coastal path; going south from the pier brings you past superb views of Capel Island and its never-completed lighthouse. The path leads on to to an abandoned signal tower dating back to 1803, built to warn of invaders. Beside it is an EIRE 21 sign, one of 80 around the country placed in 1943 during the Second World War.

BY CAR: 23 minutes from Youghal. Take R634 past the front strand. Continue for approx. 4km before turning left onto R633. Continue for 8km and turn left at Ballymacoda. Follow this road 6km to the pier at Knockadoon. Parking above the pier.

DEEP WATER • GREAT VIEWS • COASTAL PATH

GRID REF: X 09168 70332
GOOGLE MAPS REF:
51.88586, -7.86713

⑰ SIMON'S COVE

COUNTY CORK

**There are two coves for the price of
one here at the hidden Simon's Cove: in
the main cove, smooth giant rocks form
beautiful curved shapes. The pebble
beach quickly gets to a nice depth for
swimming and the high rocks create a
cove that's interesting to explore, both
for swimming and climbing its walls.
Across the rocks, a second small shale
beach tucked beneath the rock pavement
is perfect for jumping at high water.**

Few swimmers know about this hidden
bay at the end of the single-track road from
Courtmacsherry. Fewer still take the walk along
the shoreline trail to the right, squeezing past
the front of the house and down the narrow
path onto the tessellated rocks along the shore.

It leads to a pavement of flat black rock, which
abruptly drops away to reveal a curve of shale
forming a tiny beach. A narrow channel from
the sea between the high black rocks fills this
tiny bay. As you look from above, the rock pool
seems to open out like a fan as the water flows
in in the rising tide.

This womb-like pool is sheltered by the high
rocks around and, while children play safely
contained, strong swimmers may slip out
through this funnel between the rocks and
swim along the coast in the open sea. At high
water, this is a great place for jumping and
diving and children will enjoy scouring the
rock pools in search of sea urchins and crabs.
Return to the main cove where there is a
high path to the left of the beach which leads
around the cliffs to Butlerstown Cove: a lovely
walk on good-weather days.

This is a lovely place to come on the opposite
side of Clonakilty Bay, away from the popular
Inchydoney strand.

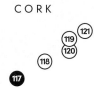

CORK

117

118

119
120

121

AT A GLANCE

117 SIMON'S COVE

A small cove 6km south of Clonakilty with smooth rocks to scramble over plus a second rock pool just a short walk around the shore where, at high water, one can jump from the rocks.

BY CAR: 1 hour 10 minutes from Cork city. Take N40 and then N71 south west to Clonakilty. Head east from Clonakilty and turn right onto the Old Timoleague Road. Follow the shore past Deasy's Bar. The road goes left, away from the coast. Turn right at the next crossroads. Continue along this road, looking out for the sign to Simon's Cove. This single-track road runs for 1.5 km down to the cove where there is a small turning circle beside a modern stone house.

FAMILY FRIENDLY • JUMPING WITH CARE

GRID REF: W 42934 38221
GOOGLE MAPS REF:
51.59397, -8.82374

118 SANDYCOVE ISLAND

Here you may meet with seasoned marathon swimmers. Do a lap of the island or simply laze in the sheltered waters between the island and mainland.

Close to Kinsale, Sandycove Island lies almost two hundred metres from the shore and is home to a herd of wild goats. The circumnavigation of the island is approximately eighteen hundred metres, making it the perfect training ground for distance aspirants. There is a great feeling of achievement on completing a journey but note: **this is suitable only for strong swimmers.** On the far side of the island, you will be exposed to rougher waters and strong currents. Never swim alone, and seek local knowledge on tides and conditions.

BY CAR: 45 minutes from Cork city. Take N27 towards Cork Airport, then take R600 through Kinsale. After the bridge, look for the signs to Sandycove on your left. At the end of the road, a small parking area gives easy access to the slipway.

EASY ACCESS • ISLAND SWIM • POPULAR WITH MARATHON SWIMMERS

GRID REF: W 63862 47284
GOOGLE MAPS REF:
51.67693, -8.52403

119 MYRTLEVILLE

Not far from Cork city, Myrtleville is a popular bay. You might meet some channel aspirants enjoying the water. With smooth, deep sand, the horseshoe-shaped bay attracts families and swimmers all through the year but it shelves quite quickly so keep an eye on your smaller swimmers. During the winter, you might want to hop in the beachside sauna for a warm-up between dips or walk the coastal path, past Bunnyconnellan Restaurant (closed) and on to Fountainstown Beach.

BY CAR: 33 minutes from Cork city. Take N28 to Carrigaline. At Shannonpark roundabout, take the second exit onto R612. At the roundabout, take the second exit; at the next roundabout, take the first exit onto Cork Road. Continue on this road till you cross the bridge. At the next roundabout, turn left for 2km, then turn right for Myrtleville. Park along the roadside under the sign for Bunnyconnellan bar and restaurant.

STEEPLY SHELVING • POPULAR

GRID REF: W 79680 58945
GOOGLE MAPS REF:
51.78273, -8.29540

Robert's Cove

(120) ROBERT'S COVE

Forty minutes from Cork city, Robert's Cove feels a world away. Out into the countryside, the approach road brings you straight down to this sheltered cove, which nestles between two tall grassy headlands. To your right, the road sweeps pleasingly around past the two pubs, the Harbour Bar and Roberts Cove Inn, and a quirky building – a former coastguard cottage – with the cutest bay window overlooking the bay. The beach is gently shelving and, if you arrive at low tide, you might take a long walk across the pristine sand, but this deep inlet still provides plenty of shelter from the open sea. A holiday park up on the left headland makes this a busy spot in the height of summer.

BY CAR: 40 minutes from Cork city. Take N40 and then N28 towards Carrigaline. At Shannonpark roundabout, take the second exit onto R611/Cork Road. At the roundabout, take the second exit; at the next roundabout, take the second exit and drive through the town. Where the road bends to the right, stay straight and go up Church Hill. Follow this for approximately 9km, then turn left onto L3210 at T-junction. Follow this for another 6km to Robert's Cove. (Watch out for the sharp left-hand bend after about 4km.) Public parking on the right.

POPULAR IN THE SUMMER • FAMILY FRIENDLY

GRID REF: W 78469 54785
GOOGLE MAPS REF:
51.74529, -8.31255

(121) WHITE BAY BEACH (CUAN BÁN)

A real treat, this beautiful strand requires a little effort. From the hilltop car park, it's a 1km walk along a well-maintained footpath. Blackberries line the way in autumn and as you round the first corner you are treated to views across to Cobh and Cork city beyond. Soon you'll see the beach lying below you. Even on a grey day, it's a tantalising sight. Here, by the entrance to the Port of Cork, you can swim and watch yachts and all manner of craft make their way into and from the port. If you feel a little chilly after your swim, the hike back up to the car park is a good warmer!

BY CAR: 47 minutes from Cork city. Take N8 and then N25 east. At Lake View roundabout, take third exit onto R630. Continue for 15km before turning right onto Trabolgan. The car park is 1km along this road on the right. Walk 1km from car park down to beach.

STEEP WALK • GREAT VIEWS

GRID REF: W 82723 61782
GOOGLE MAPS REF:
51.80848, -8.25125

⑫ LOUGH HYNE

COUNTY CORK

Until 4,000 years ago, Lough Hyne was a freshwater lake; then rising sea levels swamped it with seawater. The tide flows in to fill the lough twice a day through the narrow channel on the north-eastern corner of the lake, thus creating a warm lake of oxygenated seawater, which sustains a huge variety of marine plants, animals and fish.

Sitting in a fold of hills 5km south of the market town of Skibbereen, this marine lake has a unique ecosystem. The lough is connected to the Atlantic Ocean by a narrow channel. As the tide ebbs and flows, the lake is replenished and this maintains its varied sea life. Since 1886, scientists have carried out research in experimental ecology, looking into the factors governing the distribution of marine plants and animals, making Lough Hyne one of the most studied marine sites in Europe.

CORK

At the height of the flood, the tide rushes in at speeds up to 16km/h, creating the fast-flowing water which kayakers regularly paddle out into. Some swimmers bring out inflatables to shoot the wild waters.

The little island outcrop on the shore facing the grand house is the preferred entry point for most swimmers. Here you can wade in down a short, wide slipway into the clear water.

On Castle Island in the centre of the lake are the ancient ruins of Cloghan Castle. According to local legend, King Labhra Loinseach, who lived here, had the ears of a donkey! The swim out around the island and back is approximately fifteen hundred metres. The rapids are to be found past the left of Castle Island in the north-eastern corner of the lake. Lough Hyne is suitable for a variety of levels: you might meet grandparents introducing their grandchildren to the water.

The lake is surrounded by woodland and has a magical air. A nature trail takes you on a steep walk up through the woods of Knockomagh Hill overlooking the lough. There are two loops, one north and one south, and from the south loop one can also reach the summit, from where there are grandstand views of west Cork and out to the Atlantic Ocean.

ABOVE Lough Hyne
LEFT Barley Cove

AT A GLANCE

122 LOUGH HYNE

Swim in the clear briny waters of this sea lough, take a long swim around Castle Island or play in the strong-moving flow of 'The Rapids' during the ebb and flow tides. With its abundant sea life, it is well worth bringing a mask and snorkel for your visit here. This is home to the Lough Hyne Lappers, an unofficial group of open-water swimmers who boast among their numbers the first man to complete the Oceans Seven (a challenge to swim seven of the major sea crossings, including the English and North channels). There is room to park near this slipway and a picnic area.

BY CAR: 15 minutes from Skibbereen. Take R595 toward Baltimore and after a few kilometres a left turn is signed to Lough Hyne. This leads down to the parking at the edge of the lake. Turn left and drive along the lake shore to the outcrop and slipway.

FAMILY FRIENDLY • SCENIC WALK • SNORKELLING • BOATS OR CANOES • SWIM TO THE ISLAND

GRID REF: W 09528 28872
GOOGLE MAPS REF:
51.50598, -9.30384

123 TRAGUMNA BAY

Within striking distance of Lough Hyne, Tragumna Bay is a narrow and steep inlet. At high water you won't even see the sand, as the sea comes right up to the wall. A great belly of rock sits in the centre of the bay. A Blue Flag beach, it is fairly sheltered and gets quickly to a good depth for swimming. Snorkel around the rocks and see the variety of animals that live here.

Only 1.5km away, on the headland, is the Oceans Plastic Project. Founded in 2017, they work with transition-year students from local schools, gathering and researching the plastics washed up on our shores. Using these plastics, students make artworks and look at ways to reduce plastic consumption, a worthy endeavour.

BY CAR: 12 minutes from Skibbereen. Take R596, 3.7km. Turn right at Lake Cross, 2km then turn left. 2.5km brings you to Tragumna Beach.

FAMILY FRIENDLY • POPULAR • TOILETS • LIFEGUARDED IN SUMMER

GRID REF: W 12194 28505
GOOGLE MAPS REF:
51.50278, -9.26553

124 TRALISPEEN COVE

Only a few minutes from Tragumna is the lovely Tralispeen Cove. Sheltered by the headlands either side, this small beach is a little gem tucked in Tragumna Bay. The clear water gets to swimming depth quickly and, like many places along this coast, you can explore the rocky walls for sea life, including anemones and starfish. At 1km 'as the swimmer swims' from Tragumna beach, strong swimmers may enjoy a longer point-to-point swim, following the craggy cliffs in towards Tragumna. There are a few houses here that any swimmer would wish to own! Not one for campervans as the road is very narrow, winding and steep.

BY CAR: 14 minutes from Skibbereen. Take R595/Baltimore Road for 2.3km. Turn left and continue for 2.6km before turning right. Continue for 2.5km to the cove. Beachside parking.

NO FACILITIES • FAMILY FRIENDLY • NARROW AND WINDING APPROACH ROAD

GRID REF: W 11247 28016
GOOGLE MAPS REF:
51.49820, -9.27887

(125) DROMADOON PIER

Perfect for pier jumping at high water, this is a local favourite. Just over the headland from Tralispeen Cove, pretty Dromadoon houses a tiny beach beside the pier. At high water, there is depth enough for jumping and diving. At the pier, a converted stone boathouse enjoys the best view across turquoise waters to Bullock Island, 500m away. For a distance swim, you could aim for the stony isthmus, known as ' the coosh' which connects the island to the mainland. The island is privately owned but may have a history of pirates and smuggling! Dromadoon is a great spot to launch a kayak and explore the nooks and crannies around the coast – as always, check weather conditions before heading out.

BY CAR: 13 minutes from Skibbereen. Take R595 for 1.5km. At the roundabout, take the second exit onto R595/Baltimore Road. After 2km, turn left and continue for 4.5km to the pier. Limited parking.

FAMILY FRIENDLY • JUMPING AT HIGH TIDE

GRID REF: W 10762 28048
GOOGLE MAPS REF:
51.49842, -9.28546

Tralispeen Cove

(126) BARLEY COVE

A pristine swathe of pale golden sand tucked in between Mizen Head and Brow Head, the two most southerly points of mainland Ireland, Barley Cove is reached via a unique floating walkway. With its extensive sand dunes – formed, amazingly, by a tidal wave caused by the Lisbon earthquake in 1755 – this stunning strand attracts visitors from around the world.

The little beach tucked to the left side of the main strand is tantalisingly close but take great care is you approach as here the river flows out, creating strong currents. If you walk at low tide, be aware that the water may flood back in quickly.

BY CAR: 50 minutes from Skibbereen. Take N71 and then R592 to Schull (23km). Continue on R592 for 9km to Toormore. Continue onto R591 for 6.5km to Goleen. Turn right and continue for 4.5km, and then turn left. The parking area is 0.5km along. Walk from to the floating walkway. (Walkway may be closed in winter.)

BEAUTIFUL VIEWS • LIFEGUARDED IN SUMMER • RIVER CURRENTS

GRID REF: V 76672 25455
GOOGLE MAPS REF:
51.46918, -9.77432

⑫⑦ GLANMORE LAKE

COUNTY KERRY

Slip into tranquil waters from the tree-shaded lake shore to swim through the reflections of the towering Caha Mountains, weave around tiny rock islands with trees perched atop, growing in impossibly little soil. Climb onto the larger island, built as a crannog. Its stone hermitage is now overgrown, but the little building calls out to be explored.

Seen at its best looking down from the Healy Pass, Glanmore is one of the nicest lake swims on the Beara Peninsula. Set at the base of the steep slopes of Lackabane Mountain, with trees reaching up to the sky, it could be deep in the Canadian wilderness. On the near side, the road follows the lake shore. Quiet and surrounded by trees, there is ample opportunity to swim and plenty of places for skinny-dipping.

On a calm day, the lake waters act as a mirror, reflecting the Caha Mountains and broken only by the occasional trout jumping, spreading concentric rings out across the surface. Slipping into the lake, you realise it is alive with tiny insects flitting along the surface: it is these the trout are jumping for. They move away as you pass. You may want to swim out to one of the many little islets dotted through the lake, making your way from one to the next. Check out the largest, a crannóg on which there is an almost overgrown stone building that once housed sheltering animals.

Walkers will enjoy spending a few days exploring the area and there is a range of degrees of difficulty, from rambling the lake shore to venturing deeper into the Caha Mountains. Josie's Lakeview House Restaurant serves snacks, lunch and dinner daily. The Beara Peninsula lies between the Kenmare River to the north and Bantry Bay to the south; the Caha and Slieve Miskish Mountains run down its centre. The northern part of the peninsula is in County Kerry and the rest in County Cork. Glanmore Lake is in Kerry, close to the county border.

KERRY   CORK

RIGHT Glanmore Lake

AT A GLANCE

127 GLANMORE LAKE

The pristine Glanmore Lake has many tiny rock islands, a crannog and trout. Across from the lake, the sheer slopes of Lackabane Mountain rise up, pine trees stretching towards the sun. Enjoy the scenery as you wind along the riverbank on the way from Lauragh.

BY CAR: 36 minutes from Kenmare. Cross the bridge over the Kenmare River and turn right onto R571. This junction has an astounding 20 signs so don't even try to read them! From Lauragh, take R574 Healy Pass road, past the old pub, An Síbín. Turn left, following the signs for Josie's Lakeview House Restaurant. Continue on this narrow road, climbing farther into the mountains. Every so often a small pointer for Josie's affirms you are not lost. As you drop down and pass the entrance to Josie's, the first view of the lake will appear. Drive down to the junction where a second road follows the lake shore and choose your spot.

SCENIC WALK • SECLUDED • SKINNY-DIPPING • ISLANDS • NEARBY HOSTEL AND RESTAURANT

GRID REF: V 77391 55706
GOOGLE MAPS REF:
51.73856, -9.77142

128 GLENGARRIFF BLUE POOL

A river swim in this traditional swimming spot, described as 'a magical harbour hidden in the middle of Glengarriff'. Surrounded by woods, it could be easily missed. Beside Quills Woollen Market signs point to the Blue Pool. From the ferry jetty, follow the path round to Deirdre's Lookout, approximately 200m. With views of this natural harbour out to Garinish, here's the spot to enjoy a swim.

Spend a day here taking in the woodland walks in Glengarriff Nature Reserve, look for seals along the coast or take the ferry to Garinish Island to wander their famous gardens. The island's particular microclimate allows many exotic plants to flourish and the views from the Martello tower are little rivalled.

BY CAR: 1 hour 5 minutes from Killarney. Take N71 south through Kenmare and on to Glengarriff. The Blue Pool Amenity Area is next to Quills Woollen Market in the centre of town. Here you can catch the Blue Pool Ferry for a visit to Garinish Island.

WOODLAND WALKS • SEAL SPOTTING • DEEP WATER

GRID REF: V 93108 56255
GOOGLE MAPS REF:
51.74888, -9.54859

129 AGHABEG PIER

This secluded little harbour is tucked in an inlet on Bantry Bay, looking across towards Bere Island. This quiet pier affords a lovely exploration around the rocks of this natural harbour. The pier has a small set of steps to the outside or you can carefully wade in off the slipway. As with all harbours, be aware that sailing and fishing boats use these regularly. Good swimmer etiquette is to look out for boats, move to the shallows and keep your distance. Never swim behind a boat where crew will not see you.

Best to swim an hour before high water. Watch out for hidden rocks.

BY CAR: 1 hour 30 minutes from Killarney. Take N71 south through Kenmare and on to Glengarriff. Turn right onto R572 for 24km and then turn left onto Boher. Continue onto Bank and follow down to the small harbour. Limited parking.

WORKING HARBOUR • BEST ONE HOUR BEFORE HIGH WATER • HIDDEN ROCKS

GRID REF: V 76052 46800
GOOGLE MAPS REF:
51.66041, -9.79241

Aghabeg Pier

(130) SANDMOUNT BAY BEACH

The rocky shoreline calls for swimmers to use shoes and stretches the term 'beach', with little sand to be had. However, the views across the clean water to the eastern end of Bere Island and the fact that it is tucked away off the main tourist trail give it an appeal. A low wall runs along the edge of the single-track road, protecting it from the winter seas. Hop over this wall and take a dip in the fresh Bantry Bay waters. If you are visiting this area between July and December, Bere Island Sea Safari runs regular trips. Porpoises, seals, dolphins and whales are regularly spotted on the 90-minute tour.

BY CAR: 25 minutes from Glengarriff. Take R572 west for 25km through Arigole and on. Turn left onto L8953/Sandmount. Continue for 1.5km to the beach.

ROCKY • WILDLIFE

GRID REF: V 75413 46371
GOOGLE MAPS REF:
51.65713, -9.80098

⓭ BALLYDONEGAN BEACH

COUNTY CORK

Viewed from above, the bank of white sand at Ballydonegan Bay on the Beara Peninsula looks as though it has flowed down the hillside. Deep and soft, this strange ore-type sand has been carried down by the small river from the copper mines above Allihies and stands out against the rugged coastline and barren hillside behind. Nearing the tip of the peninsula, this beautiful beach seems to be at the end of the world, with sun glinting on wave crests on the shimmering ocean beyond.

The village of Allihies stands on the hillside above the rugged splendour of the beach and Ballydonegan Bay. Welcoming, with vibrant, painted buildings and a relaxed atmosphere at the end of summer, you are drawn to this little oasis, which hugs the hillside.

Dotted around are the remains of the copper-mining industry: stone buildings with curiously shaped chimneys, balanced on impossibly small ridges climbing towards the top of the mountain. Below, the water reaches from pale blue shallows to the deep blue-grey of the ocean and Dursey Island is visible to the west.

To the right of the beach, leading up to the pier, the stark white concrete sea-defence wall provides shelter and seating and reflects the sun's warmth.

The water shelves steeply to a good depth for swimming and several small groups of rocks are scattered along the beach. As you swim, watch for the pinnacles of rocks close to the pier, which are hidden at high tide. You might be swimming in deep water then suddenly come across a small reef. They make great diving platforms: climb onto one and find yourself standing tall, knees out of the water, then execute your stylish dive back into the deeper water.

Spend the day here, picnicking and swimming below the town. The small river to the left of the strand provides hours of entertainment for children. Take in some of the local walking trails, signposted in Allihies, and finish the day enjoying the last of the evening sunshine sipping a beer outside O'Neill's bar on the main street.

CORK

RIGHT Ballydonegan Beach

AT A GLANCE

131 BALLYDONEGAN BEACH

The beach at Ballydonegan Bay sits 1.4km below the brightly painted town of Allihies, a deep swathe of white sand, stark against the grey-green land and turquoise sea. To the right, the pale concrete bank of sea-defence wall creates a suntrap for beach goers, its tall steps providing seating close to the water's edge. There are some **strong currents** here so stay close to the beach and swim parallel to shore.

BY CAR: following the Ring of Beara, a 148km driving and cycle route from Kenmare, Allihies is at the far west of the peninsula. Take R571 from Kenmare towards Eyeries, then R575 to Allihies. The beach lies below the town.

FAMILY FRIENDLY • CAMPING • HOSTELS AND RENTAL ACCOMMODATION • GOOD FOOD • SCENIC WALKS • STRONG CURRENTS

GRID REF: V 57465 44261
GOOGLE MAPS REF:
51.63209, -10.05797

132 EYERIES PIER

Down a long, narrow laneway, it's mostly the locals that know of this spot so it's not subject to the hordes the popular beaches get on good days. But it's no less a superb swim spot! Set on the Beara Way walking trail, you might say hello to the occasional dog walker but, in general, you should find this beautifully serene. Steps lead down from the generous pier and the cove is sheltered by the rock outcrop opposite. The water is perfectly clear and brims with sea life.

BY CAR: 50 minutes from Kenmare. Take R571 along Kenmare Bay for 34.5km. Pass through Lauragh and Ardgroom. Continue for 3.5km on R571. At the fork, veer right. After 0.5km, turn left. Continue for 2.5km and then turn right down the narrow road as you enter Eyeries and follow this winding lane down to the pier. Watch out for potholes!

SECLUDED • LIMITED PARKING ABOVE PIER

GRID REF: V 64222 51414
GOOGLE MAPS REF:
51.69903, -9.96472

133 TEERNEA BAY BEACH

The first of two little beaches in this far west part of the Beara Peninsula, Teernea has a small slipway leading down to the strand of mixed stone and sand. On sunny days, the water takes on a turquoise hue and with the hills of the Iveragh Peninsula rising out of the sea across the bay, it feels beautifully wild and remote. A whitewashed building provides a changing area; tucked under the high bank it gives excellent shelter from wind and rain. Patches of stones line the shore here.

BY CAR: 1 hour 30 minutes from Kenmare. Take R571 from Kenmare towards Eyeries, then R575 to Allihies (14km). Turn left at the beach to stay on R575 for 4km and then turn right onto R572. Continue for 5.5km, then turn right at Beara Holiday Homes. In less than 0.5km, the beaches are on your right.

COVERED CHANGING AREA • RUGGED BEACH • CALM CONDITIONS ONLY

GRID REF: V 52477 42227
GOOGLE MAPS REF:
51.61367, -10.13071

Garinish Beach

(134) GARINISH BEACH

Continuing west from Allihies, heading towards Dursey, is the sheltered Garinish Beach. The shallow waters of Garinish Bay and the surrounding rock outcrops make this a natural harbour and during the summer you may see a few sailing boats moored here. Dursey Island is a short boat trip from the harbour around the headland. These waters have strong currents but the beach here is enclosed in a natural harbour, protected from these currents.

During the summer you can also take the trip to Dursey Island on Ireland's only cable car, refurbished in 2023.

BY CAR: 1 hour 30 minutes from Kenmare. Take R571 from Kenmare towards Eyeries, then R575 to Allihies (14km). Turn left at the beach to stay on R575 for 4km before turning right onto R572. Continue for 5.5km and turn right at Beara Holiday Homes. Garinish beach and harbour are at the end of this road, past Teernea.

GRID REF: V 52206 42659
GOOGLE MAPS REF:
51.61745, -10.13531

Eyeries Pier

(135) FORGE COVE AND AMPHITHEATRE

COUNTY CORK

As you travel west along the R571, the Ring of Beara gives unparalleled views of Coulagh Bay to the north and the Miskish Mountains to the south. Along this road on the approach to Cod's Head on the north-west tip of the Beara Peninsula. Looking back along the craggy coastline, there are several places to park. Climb the low wall between the road and the shore and scramble down for a dip. As the road drops down from the magnificent mountain drive back towards the shore, Forge Cove, nestled in a tight sweeping curve of the road, is breathtaking in its simple beauty.

The deep, crystal-clear water is hard to resist on a hot day and utterly refreshing after a long drive on these twisting and undulating roads. A long narrow slipway runs down the centre of the pebble beach into the water. A few rowboats rest on the beach at low tide.

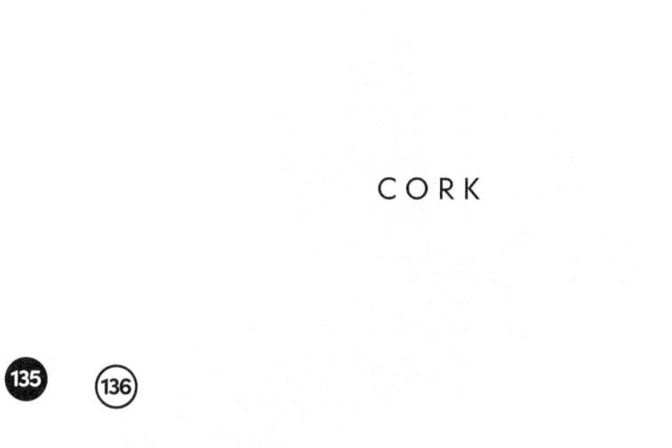

From here, observe how the road just travelled seems precariously shored up with drystone walling on the opposite side of the cove.

Climb around the rocks to the left of this delightful little bay where there is a narrow cleft creating a channel that cuts through the rocks behind the pier. The cove quickly gets deep, and one can enjoy a leisurely swim.

For the adventure swimmer who likes challenging conditions, just a few hundred metres along this road is the 'Amphitheatre'. This deep bowl of rock and churning sea is at its best at mid to low tide. The water writhes and churns, creating whirlpools and eddies as the swell plays around the rock. Don't attempt to swim in the bowl of the Amphitheatre itself.

For strong swimmers only: climb along the right-hand side of the amphitheatre where a straight and narrow inlet gives the best access. Here, it is possible to jump from the rocks into deep water. The visibility is good and the rocks are stepped, making it easy for an agile swimmer to climb out. The swirl of the water is immensely powerful in the 'amphitheatre' itself, even in flat-calm conditions so care should be taken not to venture too close.

The steep sides of this bowl of rock provide shelter from the wind and create a suntrap where one can spend several hours simply drinking in the sounds of the swell and the tide.

ABOVE AND LEFT
Forge Cove and Amphitheatre

AT A GLANCE

135 FORGE COVE AND AMPHITHEATRE

Forge Cove: swim in the crystal-clear waters of this roadside cove where turquoise hues light up in the autumn sunlight at this pretty little bay.

BY CAR: 1 hour 7 minutes from Kenmare. Take R751 west along the northern shore of the Beara Peninsula, 42km. Shortly after the turn for Eyeries, turn right onto R575 towards Allihies, 12km. As the road drops down and sweeps around close to the water's edge, the beach and slipway are revealed. Parking is on the roadside verge.

ROADSIDE PARKING ONLY • NO FACILITIES • BOATS • ROCKS AND ROCK POOLS • EASY ACCESS

GRID REF: V 57658 46556
GOOGLE MAPS REF:
51.65389, -10.05799

Amphitheatre: at mid to low tide this amphitheatre is revealed, the tide washing in and out, creating whirlpools and eddies. Climb over the rocks to the right of the amphitheatre. Here an inlet deep enough to jump from the stepped rocks provides safe access for strong swimmers and for climbing out again. **Not recommended to venture into the bowl itself** and

great care should be taken as, even on calm days, the effect is somewhat like a washing machine.

BY CAR: from Forge Cove (above), drive on a few bends in the road into the townland of Dooneen on R575 to Allihies. The curious stone theatre is visible over the low wall. A few hundred metres on, a lay-by on the left gives room to park a couple of cars. Walk back down the road, over the stone wall and climb down to the deep bowl of stone.

ADVANCED ADVENTURE SWIM, STRONG SWIMMERS ONLY • JUMPING AND DIVING WITH CARE

GRID REF: V 57754 46287
GOOGLE MAPS REF:
51.65217, -10.05892

136 GORTNAKILLA PIER

Another west-coast fishing pier is super for a lazy dip in good conditions. As you look out from its narrow channel-like inlet on the southern shores of Bantry Bay, this rustic little pier has a simple charm. Passing old stone cottages on your way to shore makes one think of the lives that were played out here in the past. **Only suitable in calm conditions.**

BY CAR: 26 minutes from Bantry. Take N71 towards Clashduff. After 2km, turn right. After a further 2km, turn right and then left to continue along the coast road for 14km. Gortnakilla Pier is signposted to the right. Very limited parking at the pier, so best to park here at the roadside layby and walk down the narrow track to the pier, about 700 metres.

WORKING PIER • BEST IN CALM CONDITIONS • LIMITED PARKING

GRID REF: V 82431 41302
GOOGLE MAPS REF:
51.61235, -9.69819

Gortnakilla Pier

ⓥ DERRYNANE

COUNTY KERRY

Viewed from the road above, Derrynane Beach, once notorious as a smugglers' port, makes the swimmer itch to get down to it. The road is long and winding and seems to take you far past the first tantalising view, but persevere and follow the signs for Derrynane House. These will eventually lead you down to the shore and this gorgeous string of beaches.

Walking from the car park over the grassy bank, you will find the beaches laid out in front: a series of sandy coves, each a different size and shape. The water virtually calls out for you to run down the strand and dive right in.

 KERRY

Picture-perfect, the white sandy beaches curve around between the scattered rocks where you can happily while away an entire day swimming and rock-pooling in this natural harbour.

As you walk along the strand, you'll easily find a private space, sheltered from the wind and away from other visitors, behind one of the several rock outcrops. Take care at the largest stretch of beach as it is prone to **strong currents**, but there are plenty of coves and bays to explore. Sunsets here are unparalleled, bathing the cove in pink and purple hues.

Derrynane House, the grounds of which lead down to the beach, is the ancestral home of Daniel O'Connell, 'The Liberator', the 19th-century politician who championed the cause of Catholic Emancipation. The oldest surviving part of the house was built in 1825 and the chapel was added in 1844, modelled on the ruined monastery chapel on the nearby Abbey Island. The house and gardens were opened to the public in 1967. Take in some of the history of the area and make the most of the views by walking the short distance to Abbey Island, accessible at low tide, where O'Connell's wife, Mary, is buried.

Before leaving this magical place, call in at The Blind Piper in Caherdaniel for a pint and a sandwich to fuel the onward journey.

Derrynane Beach

AT A GLANCE

137 DERRYNANE

A beautiful natural harbour contained between Abbey Island to the west and Lamb's Head to the south, this series of separate beaches provides great bathing, best for sunsets.

At the western end of the beach, a spit of sand leads onto Abbey Island and the remains of the eighth-century St Finian's Abbey.

BY CAR: 8 minutes from Caherdaniel in the south-western corner of the Iveragh Peninsula on N70/Ring of Kerry route. At Caherdaniel, look for signs to Derrynane Trá. Passing The Blind Piper pub, continue for 2km. At the fork keep right, continue 1.2km to the beach parking.

Continue along the twisting road, past Derrynane House. Drive to the large car park close to the shore. If visiting Derrynane House, adult admission is €5, family €13 (correct at time of writing).

FAMILY FRIENDLY • POPULAR • STRONG CURRENTS • SCENIC WALK • STUNNING SUNSETS

GRID REF: V 52582 58489
GOOGLE MAPS REF:
51.76021, -10.13745

138 BALLINSKELLIGS

Ballinskelligs – 'the place of the craggy rock' – is a Blue Flag beach but it never gets really busy, as it is tucked out of the way on the Iveragh Peninsula. The 'craggy rocks' refer to the Skellig Islands – Skellig Rock Great (or Sceilg Mhichíl) and Skellig Rock Little – which were home in the sixth century to monks.

The beach is at the western end of Ballinskelligs Bay. The 1km of soft white sand shelves gradually and has clear, sheltered waters. The ruins of MacCarthy Mór's castle sit on a narrow isthmus that juts out into the bay facing the beach.

Watch the chocolate-making process in the nearby Skelligs Chocolate factory or take a boat trip to visit Sceilg Mhichíl : this ancient monastic settlement is a UNESCO World Heritage site.

BY CAR: 1 hour 30 minutes from Kenmare. Take N70/Ring of Kerry south-west for 65km through Waterville. Turn left onto R567. After 6km, take R566 towards Ballinskelligs and follow the signs to the beach and car park.

FAMILY FRIENDLY • POPULAR

GRID REF: V 43484 65503
GOOGLE MAPS REF:
51.82095, -10.27262

139 LOUGH CARAGH

In the Reeks District and Killarney National Park, Caragh is a pristine lake perfect for swimming, kayaking and fishing. This small slip could be easily missed, tucked under the trees on the lake's northern shores. Spanning 8km, it gives you plenty of scope for whatever distance you enjoy swimming. For the best views of the lake, and on a good day a complete panorama taking in the MacGillycuddy's Reeks and the Dingle Peninsula, take a hike in Caragh Lake Forest. This is graded strenuous; the lake trail is 1.7km with a steep extra 410m Mountain Spur trail, which affords the best of the views.

BY CAR: 40 minutes from Tralee. Take N70 for 32km, passing through Castlemaine. Turn left onto L7508 signed Tooreennasliggaun and continue for 1km. Turn right and travel 225m. Look for the public access to the lake on the left opposite impressive gates in the stone wall. Very limited parking on the roadside.

LAKE SWIM • SCENIC • LIMITED PARKING • KAYAKING

GRID REF: V 72720 92916
GOOGLE MAPS REF:
52.07387, -9.85736

Ballinskelligs

⑭⓪ GLANLEAM

COUNTY KERRY

Valentia Island's own tourism website states that it is easy to find and that 'the small island known as Ireland lies to the east'. This quirkiness and sense of fun draws you to Valentia. Many visitors will take the main route and arrive in the bustling centre of Knight's Town, where swimming in the harbour is popular, but for a quiet and more secluded swim, take the road north west towards Glanleam House and Gardens. From this tiny private beach, you can swim between Valentia and Beginish Island or follow the coast west towards the lighthouse.

This spot is a local secret, and you might meet someone taking to the waters for its reputed health benefits, a tradition that has been passed down through the generations.

The small beach is at the bottom of a narrow lane from the road, just metres from the entrance to Glanleam House and Gardens, an old estate dating back to the 1770s, which was home to five generations of the Knights of Kerry, who each extended the house. The subtropical gardens are a major attraction. At the beach, there are two old boathouses.

The small beach of grey sand melts into the water. Beginish Island lies directly in front of the bay; to the left along the shore is Valentia's lighthouse.

The swim to the lighthouse is approximately 1.25km and it is almost the same distance across to Beginish at its closest point. If you plan to swim to Beginish, have an accompanying kayak as the boats from Knight's Town use Tooreennasliggaun, the channel between the two islands.

At only 11km long by 5km wide, Valentia is perfect for cycling trips and the pretty and vibrant Knight's Town has plenty to offer by way of food and entertainment. The harbour area plays host to a half-marathon event at the beginning of autumn, and, with pontoons alongside the main jetty, is also popular for swimming in the summer.

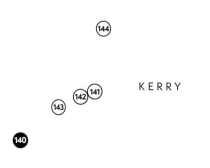

KERRY

Glanleam

AT A GLANCE

140 GLANLEAM

Bathe at this tiny bay hidden away beneath Glanleam House and Gardens or take a longer, scenic swim along the coast to the lighthouse. Rent a refurbished boathouse for a weekend to get away from it all.

BY CAR: 1 hour 45 minutes from Tralee. Follow N70/Ring of Kerry and then R565 to Portmagee and cross the bridge onto Valentia Island. Follow the road towards Knight's Town. At Castletown, turn left and cut across the island following the signs for Glanleam House and Gardens. The beach is down a small slipway just before the house and gardens. Alternatively, take N70/Ring of Kerry to Cahersiveen, then follow the signs for the ferry.

THE FERRY to Knight's Town is a five-minute trip and, at time of writing, a single trip for a car costs €11; return €15. The ferry service from Cahersiveen runs during the summer season until October.

FAMILY FRIENDLY • SECLUDED • SCENIC SWIM

GRID REF: V 40680 77144
GOOGLE MAPS REF:
51.92402, -10.31700

141 DOOKS STRAND

Only 12km from Killorglin, this quiet beach is a dream. The nearest parking is at Cromane beach (signed from the N70/Ring of Kerry): walk past the golf clubhouse along a laneway to the beach.

When the tide is full, the wooden pontoon provides a platform to dive from or simply laze on to warm up on a sunny day before you swim back to shore. Even with the houses behind, the beach does not feel overlooked and has an incredible stillness.

BY CAR: 40 minutes from Killarney. Take N71 onto N72/Ring of Kerry. At Killorglin continue onto N70/Ring of Kerry, heading west for 10km. At Caragh Bridge, turn right, signed Dooks, and continue for 2km. Look for the curved, low wall and entrance to a private laneway with a post box on the wall. This private road has ramps. Follow it down to the next right turn. This brings you to a cul-de-sac, where a sandy track leads onto the beach.

BEAUTIFUL WALK • SECLUDED

GRID REF: V 67794 93521
GOOGLE MAPS REF:
52.07779, -9.92966

142 ROSSBEIGH

A large land spit that juts out northwards into the bay, Rossbeigh has sands on all sides. Facing Dooks to the right and out to sea on the left, whichever way the wind is blowing, the other side will have some protection. At its widest, it is mostly sand with a narrow strip of dunes.

There are plenty of holiday rentals within an easy walk to the beach and with horse riding available locally, it is a great base for a family holiday.

It is easily accessible, with ample car parking and concrete paths that lead to the shore. When the tide is in, there is very little sand, but at mid to low tide there is plenty of room for children to play or horse riders to gallop along the strand.

BY CAR: 45 minutes from Killarney. Take N72 to Killorglin and from there N70/Ring of Kerry to Glenbeigh. Turn right onto R564, signposted for the beach.

POPULAR FAMILY BEACH • GOOD FACILITIES • SWIMMING AND SURFING

GRID REF: V 64661 91706
GOOGLE MAPS REF:
52.06073, -9.97409

(143) KELLS BAY

There's a super weekend hideaway for a young family in this pretty little fishing harbour. The small beach is contained between the harbour wall and a rocky headland, and you can buy crabs for supper direct from the boats. A more exposed cove on the other side of the harbour wall provides a bit more seclusion and challenge for more experienced swimmers. Accommodation is facing the beach with a few caravans and glamping pods (Kells Beach Camping). As you approach the beach beyond Kells Bay Gardens, the road drops steeply down and it feels like you are entering a rainforest, as the trees and plants thicken, finally leading you to the harbour and beach.

BY CAR: 40 minutes from Killorglin. Take N70/Ring of Kerry west for 26km, passing the Gleensk Viaduct. Turn right onto L4015, signed Kells. Continue 1.5km and then turn sharp right, signed Kells Bay House and Gardens. Continue 1km, then turn left to the beach.

FAMILY FRIENDLY • BEACH CAMPSITE • GLAMPING PODS • GOOD FOOD • KAYAKING

GRID REF: V 55616 87914
GOOGLE MAPS REF:
52.02478, -10.10480

The Dooks

(144) FENIT

This popular coastal town at the mouth of Tralee Bay is home to many sea swimmers, from the regular Christmas Day swim which often sees over three hundred brave the winter waters, to a good pedigree of channel swimmers, triple crown swimmers and more. You're sure to find a swim buddy here among the Tralee Bay Swimming Club and Wild Water Adventures, who organise the Fenit Swimfest. Started in 2021, this is a weekend of swimming events for all levels.

Fenit Lighthouse is a well-known landmark and, at 1km as the crow flies from the beach, it is included in the Swimfest. Walk the full length of the beach; the coastal path brings you to the old diving platform looking across to the lighthouse.

BY CAR: 20 minutes from Tralee. Take R551 for 2.5km. At the roundabout, take the first exit onto R558. Continue for 10km into Fenit. There is a large parking area near the West End Bar.

POPULAR • FAMILY FRIENDLY • SWIMFEST EVENTS

GRID REF: Q 72694 15346
GOOGLE MAPS REF:
52.27577, -9.86653

 MINARD

COUNTY KERRY

The storm beach of Minard is considered one of the finest of its type in Ireland. Great boulders rounded by the sea and then thrown onto the shore during storms tumble down to the waters' edge. The sand is revealed only at low tide. Prominent on the hill overlooking the bay are the remains of the 16th-century Minard Castle, one of three Fitzgerald castles on the peninsula.

The Dingle Peninsula in Ireland's south west stretches 50km out into the Atlantic Ocean, with the Blasket Islands on its western tip and dominated by a spine of mountains running from Slieve Mish to Mount Brandon.

KERRY

The coastline consists of steep cliffs and many sandy beaches safe for swimming and surfing, among which Minard has a special appeal. The great sandstone boulders piled on the beach have been worn smooth over the aeons and serve as a natural barrier that prevents flooding and erosion of the fields inshore. The cliffs of Minard around the bay are made of fossilised desert sand dunes, 380 million years old.

At low tide, the beach is superb for swimming, with calm water and no strong currents. There are organised swimming lessons for local children during the summer months. A little bridge at the foot of the castle grounds is a popular children's paddling spot. At high tide, the sand will be all but submerged and it is the great stones which take centre stage.

The castle above the bay was once the stronghold of the Knights of Kerry. Cromwellian forces attempted to blow it up in 1650, placing charges at each corner. It withstood the blasts and three storeys of the rectangular tower still survive. However, the damage was such that it was no longer habitable. In more recent history, Minard is where the young Tom Crean from Anascaul enlisted with the British Navy. He was a member of three major Antarctic expeditions, under Scott and Shackleton, and earned three Polar Medals. When Crean retired from the navy, he returned to Anascaul and, with his wife, opened a pub called The South Pole Inn.

Minard Beach

AT A GLANCE

(145) MINARD

Scramble over the amazing, rounded boulders down to the beach at low tide, perfect for swimming in this gently shelving bay.

BY CAR: 45 minutes from Tralee. Take N86 to Anascaul. Minard beach and castle are about fifteen minutes' drive from Anascaul (or a two-hour walk approx. along quiet country roads). From Anascaul, head south west towards Dingle, then take the first left, signed for Inch. After 450m, turn right and follow this road to Minard Castle.

From Dingle town, take N86 east to Lispole (approx. 8km). About 2km after Lispole, turn right towards Minard. This road brings you to the beach.

SCENIC WALK • FAMILY FRIENDLY

GRID REF: V 55625 99246
GOOGLE MAPS REF:
52.12693, –10.10887

(146) LOUGH DOON

The Conor Pass is a highlight of the Dingle Peninsula. Lough Doon – known locally as Pedlar's Lake – is perfect for swimming, hidden from sight and just a short climb from the roadside car park. The only clue to its presence is the cascading waterfall seen on the approach. Climb up the unmarked path over the great slabs of granite beside the falls and pick your way over rocks to reach the small but perfectly formed lake, nestled in a small valley surrounded by tall glacial peaks. The lake gets deep quickly and, at around 200m across, makes for a fabulous mountain swim.

Take care walking over the slippery rocks. Remember that mountain lakes are notoriously cold so take your time getting in, make sure your breathing has settled and don't outstay your welcome.

BY CAR: 10 minutes from Dingle town. Take the Spa Road to the Conor Pass. After almost 9km, look for the small parking area beside the waterfall. Climb up over the rocks to the lake.

MOUNTAIN LAKE SWIM • SCENIC VIEWS

GRID REF: Q 50293 06123
GOOGLE MAPS REF:
52.18618, –10.18864

(147) WINE STRAND

Wine Strand is the smallest of three super beaches in Smerwick Harbour and is tucked in the middle, off the narrow shore road. Less than 100m across, this tiny cove still packs a punch. The rocks either side give protection and a place to scramble up and dive back in. Follow the cliff to the left of the beach for 175m and look for the narrow break on the rocks leading to a tiny harbour. From here, look east and you'll see the swathe of Gallarus Beach. To the west is another: Trá Bhéal Bán.

BY CAR: 15 minutes from Dingle town. Take R559/Slea Head Drive. Continue for 4km. Veer left following signs for Wine Strand (4km). Turn right at Tig Bhric & West Kerry Brewery, signed Wine Strand. Continue for 1km, signed. Park up on the grass and walk the sandy path onto the beach. The tiny harbour is 200m farther on with further parking.

SMALL BEACH • FAMILY FRIENDLY • ROCKS AND JUMPING WITH CARE

GRID REF: Q 36881 05661
GOOGLE MAPS REF:
52.17879, –10.38582

Wine Strand

(148) CASTLEGREGORY

It's no wonder this huge expanse of beach – 4.5km of golden sand – is nicknamed the Gold Coast of Dingle. With so much beach, even on a busy day you can get away from the crowds. You may see horse riders enjoying the soft sand as they canter along the shoreline of Tralee Bay. To the north west, the Magharees spit of land shelters the bay, dividing it from neighbouring Brandon Bay to the west. The sand dunes here are home to the rare natterjack toad and at the end of Magharees there are views to the Seven Hogs Islands.

BY CAR: 30 minutes from Dingle town. Take Spa Road onto R560 through Conor Pass (12km). Continue onto Ballyhoneen for 2.8km. As the road sweeps left it becomes Glennahoo. Continue for 6km through Stradbally. Turn left, signed Castlegregory, and continue for 2km to the town on Main Street and then Strand Street. At Fitzgerald's, take the second right onto Strand Road, from where it is 0.5km to the beach.

FAMILY FRIENDLY • HORSE-RIDING • SWIMMING • SURFING

GRID REF: Q 62571 13941
GOOGLE MAPS REF:
52.26029, -10.01334

(149) BRANDON CREEK

In strong weather, the waves drive in, crashing off the rocky walls and bouncing back on each other – not the time to swim! But in good conditions, a dive in off the slipway into the deep, clear waters is exhilarating. Enjoy the high walls towering above as you investigate the spot where it's said St Brendan set sail for 'the promised land of the saints' in AD 535. The account of his journey, and of the 14 monks who accompanied him, *Navigatio Sancti Brendani Abbatis,* gained legendary status in medieval Europe. In 1976/77, Tim Severin and five crew repeated the journey in a similar boat – a curragh – to prove it was possible and were successful in reaching Newfoundland.

BY CAR: 18 minutes from Dingle town. Take R549 north for 12.4km. Turn right, signed Brandon Creek, and continue for 1km. The road finally weaves down a sharp left-hand turn to the pier.

PIER JUMPING • LIMITED PARKING

GRID REF: Q 42369 12042
GOOGLE MAPS REF:
52.23779, -10.30998

POLLOCK HOLES

COUNTY CLARE

Step out onto the Duggerna Rock at the mouth of Kilkee's horseshoe bay and walk onto a barren and exposed landscape. Steps lead down to a pile of rounded stones and, beyond the reef, revealed at low tide is a plateau of rock, smoothed by the twice-daily ebb and flow of the sea. As the sea drops away from the rocks, the magical pools are revealed: the Pollock Holes, three good-sized pools, left full by the retreating tide and full of life.

As you slip into the still water of these sheltered pools, anemones wave their soft tentacles, stroking as you pass, in search of unseen creatures. The colourful underwater world is far removed from the hard and flat grey stone above. Even as the Atlantic rages at the edge of the reef, creating swathes of foam which blow across the pools, one can peacefully swim and snorkel, the yellows and purples of underwater plants lighting up the pale green waters.

Kilkee has been a seaside resort town for nearly two hundred years, starting with the passenger steamer service in 1816 between Limerick and Kilrush. As the town grew in popularity, the West Clare Railway was built in the late 1800s and the area has been popular ever since.

Inside the bay, the crescent-shaped beach, sheltered by the Duggerna Rock, has drawn holidaymakers since those early days. Look for the monochrome portrait of Che Guevara on the beach wall.

For the reef, continue to the end of the road and the large car park at the Diamond Rocks Café. The Pollock Holes are directly in front, revealed at low tide. If you have arrived early and need to kill some time, take a walk around the headland for spectacular views and watch the waves explode as they hit the reef. Traditionally, the nearest pool was for ladies only and the farthest was for men, but now they are mixed and increasingly popular for snorkelling.

These pools have become an institution and, although well known (and therefore busy) during summer, they are well worth the visit. Warm up in the café with scones and hot coffee after your swim.

CLARE

Pollock Holes

AT A GLANCE

(150) POLLOCK HOLES

Swim amidst the amazing sea life caught in these rock pools revealed at low tide. Follow it with the exhilarating rush of jumping from high boards along the cliffs and finish the day with a stroll along the crescent-shaped sheltered beach, all within this one bay.

BY CAR: 55 minutes from Ennis. Take N68 to Kilrush and then N67 to Kilkee. Drive through the town and at the roundabout, take L2009, signposted Coast Road. Follow this road as it winds along the western side of the bay until you reach the car park. The rocks can be slippery as you walk out. Beware of the incoming tide as the outer rocks get cut off quite quickly.

FAMILY FRIENDLY • ROCK POOLS • JUMPING WITH CARE • LOW TIDE ONLY • SNORKELLING

GRID REF: Q 88114 60139
GOOGLE MAPS REF:
52.68454, -9.66635

(151) MOUNTSHANNON

Lough Derg reaches into three counties – Clare, Galway and Tipperary – and is the third largest lough in Ireland. The name means 'bloody eye', after the father of the gods in Irish mythology, the Dagda, washed his wounded face in the lake waters. Here, beside the busy Mountshannon harbour, is a Blue Flag swimming area where you can safely enjoy the water while watching riverboats and cruisers make their way along the Shannon Blueway. Narrow concrete jetties provide easy access (**check depth before diving**) and it is lifeguarded during the summer. The lough stretches some 39km from Portumna to Killaloe. Mountshannon sits on its western shores.

BY CAR: 45 minutes from Ennis. Take R352/Tulla Road east for 42km to Mountshannon. Turn right, signed for the harbour. Plenty of parking either here or along the road.

FAMILY FRIENDLY • LIFEGUARDED IN SUMMER • POPULAR

GRID REF: R 71233 86564
GOOGLE MAPS REF:
52.92936, -8.42855

(152) GLASHEEN BEACH

A personal favourite of mine for a winter swim, this tiny beach is snuggled between two banks of rock and looks onto the mouth of the River Shannon. At only 95m across, and less at high tide, it is tiny! Steps lead down to the shore, and on a high spring tide you may find the water lapping against them. The bay shelves quite quickly and on stormy days can get very choppy. On a calm day, however, it's a lovely swim as you look up at the rocks above. A quick run back up the steps and then a warming cuppa seated at one of the stone picnic tables rounds off the swim.

BY CAR: 12 minutes from Kilkee. Take N67 south for 600m. Turn right onto Circular Road. At the roundabout, take the second exit onto R487/Church Road and continue for 3km. Turn left, signed Loop Head Drive, and continue 4.5km to the beach.

PICNIC AREA

GRID REF: Q 88280 52868
GOOGLE MAPS REF:
52.61583, -9.65048

Whitestrand

(153) WHITESTRAND AND KERINS HOLE

At 200m across and in a deep inlet protected by low cliffs on either side, this is a great place for laps. Gently shelving, it will suit all levels of swimmer and, when the tide is high and the beach almost fully covered, you can still get in the water from the wide slipway. North of Kilkee and easy to find, this strand has a hidden bonus: off to the right, approximately 300m along the cliff edge path, is the rock pool Kerins Hole. Steps lead down off the rocks and at high water you can plunge in (**always check the depth**). On a hot day, just laze on the rocks warming up until you are ready for your next dip.

BY CAR: 30 minutes from Kilkee. Take N67 north for 32 km through Miltown Malbay. Turn left onto Fintra More, L2124/Whitestrand. Some roadside parking.

FAMILY FRIENDLY • BEACH AND ROCK POOL • POPULAR

GRID REF: R 03984 80516
GOOGLE MAPS REF:
52.86719, -9.42689

(154) FLAGGY SHORE

An attractive little beach of mixed sand and stone, the low wall above the beach dotted with pebbles adds to its appeal. The clear waters shelve gently but there are stones so watch your footing. Take a walk out to the Martello tower at Finavarra Point. This is a 9km loop walk on good roads.

BY CAR: 1 hour 10 minutes from Galway city, take R336 east then turn right onto N6. At Coolagh roundabout take the first exit onto N67, stay on N67 for 33km. Turn right onto L1022/Finavarra/Flaggy Shore. Turn right, signed Russell Gallery. At the gallery, turn left and then right, signed Flaggy Shore.

ROADSIDE PARKING • GENTLY SHELVING • LOOP WALK

GRID REF: M 27364 12347
GOOGLE MAPS REF:
53.15701, -9.08626

Ballydowane,
County Waterford

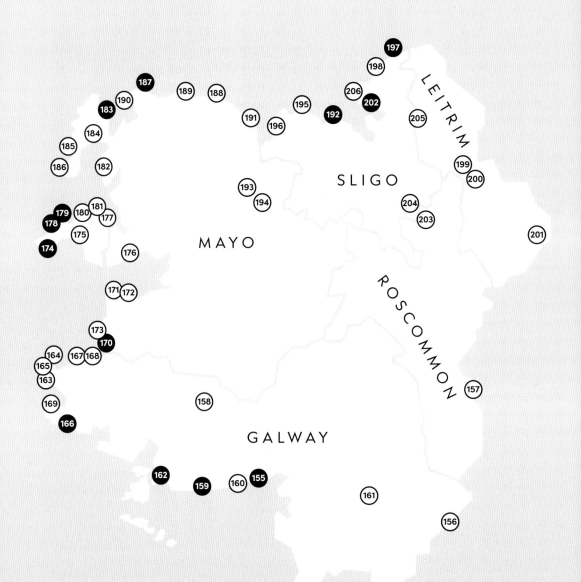

LEITRIM

SLIGO

MAYO

ROSCOMMON

GALWAY

CONNACHT

AT GALWAY CITY A SERIES of beaches run the length of the promenade all the way to the iconic diving boards at Blackrock Tower, where swimmers and divers of all ages congregate year-round and at any time of day. Journey west along this coastline and you are spoilt for choice of swimming spots. Don't miss the curious coral beach, Trá an Dóilín, in Connemara. Take a few days in Mayo for Achill Island and Belmullet before journeying inland to the freshwater loughs of Sligo, Roscommon and Leitrim.

⑮⑤ BLACKROCK DIVING TOWER

COUNTY GALWAY

From the vibrant musical bustle of Galway city's street performers and pubs, it is a short step to the hills of Connemara and the beaches of the west of Ireland. From the city centre, you can walk 2km along the promenade to Blackrock bathing area and Salthill's famous diving boards, where you will meet a population of hardy swimmers and divers who regularly fling themselves from the high board, whatever the weather.

The bathing area and boards are like a magnet, drawing young and old, and are a hive of activity as retirees mix with schoolchildren to swim and jump from the dual-aspect platforms. The boards have become a rite of passage for school leavers. On the final day of term before the summer holidays, they flock en masse to the Blackrock Diving Tower and climb the steps to charge off the highest board.

A 30-minute walk from the centre of town brings you to this iconic Galway swimming hole: Salthill's diving boards on Blackrock Tower. The walls are built at strategic angles to provide shelter from the wind for changing, and a long, low bench serves as seating. A wide crescent of steps leads down into the sea at the bathing section, behind the diving boards. A narrow staircase rises up the centre of the structure to the top diving platform where divers gather their nerve before taking the plunge.

Join the local swimmers who will happily guide you to the very best places to visit and shower you with stories of the area.

As you walk the promenade between Salthill and Galway city, look for quotes from the Nobel Prize-winning poet Seamus Heaney embedded in the walls and on the pavement, or visit the National Aquarium of Ireland, Galway Atlantaquaria, on the prom. End your day back in the vibrant city with its wide variety of restaurants and pubs with live music.

RIGHT Blackrock Diving Tower

AT A GLANCE

155 BLACKROCK DIVING TOWER

Join the locals at this popular bathing area and dive from the dual-aspect boards which have featured in several films, including Brendan Gleeson's *The Guard*.

BY CAR: 5 minutes from Galway city. Take the road towards Salthill. There is car parking at various points along the 2km promenade. The bathing area is found at the far end.

BY FOOT: from Galway city, walk along the promenade, 30 minutes approx.

FAMILY FRIENDLY • JUMPING WITH CARE • POPULAR

GRID REF: M 27199 23526
GOOGLE MAPS REF:
53.25633, -9.09238

156 PORTUMNA

A purpose-built swim area on the northern shores of Lough Derg, with two long jetties complete with ladders to get easily into the deeper water. There is also a shallow children's area. This is a popular spot, lifeguarded during the summer and close to the town. You can see the boats cruising past and into the harbour at the castle but be assured the swim area is designated. Part of the Lough Derg Blueway, there are plenty of recreation trails for kayaking, SUPing, walking and cycling. Castle Harbour has the superb Waterways Ireland toilets and showering facilities, designed for boaters and campers. You can pick up a Smartcard at local shops, An Post or order online from Waterways Ireland.

BY CAR: 1 hour 15 minutes from Galway city. Take N6 east. At Junction 16, take the exit for N6 Portumna/Loughrea. Stay on N65 for 37km to Portumna. Continue onto Shannon Road, the lakeside swimming area is signposted.

POPULAR • LIFEGUARDED IN SUMMER • PARKING • WALKS NEARBY

GRID REF: M 85914 03639
GOOGLE MAPS REF:
53.08350, -8.21106

157 JUDY'S HARBOUR

Almost halfway along the western shores of Lough Ree lies this quiet little harbour space. Perfect for a stop-off, swim and refuel with a picnic or barbecue. The shallow waters are stony but clear and offer a lovely scenic swim. Keep an eye on the left-hand shore and look for Rindoon Mill. *Rinn Dúin,* or fortified headland, was an important medieval town and it witnessed many battles and sieges between the Irish chieftains and Norman barons. At the generous car park, a large wooden shelter covers a picnic table and, with bench seating running along the three sides, it makes a perfect changing area.

BY CAR: 1 hour 30 minutes from Galway city. Take M6 to Athlone. At Junction 12, take N61 Sligo/Roscommon. Continue for 7km, passing St Brigid's GAA. Turn right. After 2km, turn right and continue 4.5km to the harbour.

FAMILY FRIENDLY WITH ACTIVITY BOARDS FOR SMALL CHILDREN • BUSY IN MAY FOR FISHING • LOCAL HONEY FOR SALE (WITH HONESTY BOX)

GRID REF: M 99671 54556
GOOGLE MAPS REF:
53.54123, -8.00652

(158) HILL OF DOON VIEWPOINT PIER

This old stone pier, topped with low-cropped grass, is a beautiful spot overlooking the western end of Lough Corrib. Full of islands, islets and crannogs – some 1,327, according to recent figures – the lough is a kayaker's dream. Take a gentle swim in this quiet spot and admire the scenery. Perhaps venture out to one of those rocky islets. The opposite tree-covered shore rises sharply out of the lake only 400m away. The pier is a short hike down from the parking lay-by over the field. Bring suitable footwear.

Hill of Doon Viewpoint Pier

BY CAR: 55 minutes from Galway city. Take N59/Clifden Road for 26.5km. At Oughterard, turn right onto Camp Street, then left onto Glann Road. Continue for 13 km, along the edge of the lough and past Derroura Woods. From the parking bay, walk down to the pier.

SECLUDED LAKE SWIM • SCENIC

GRID REF: M 03465 49346
GOOGLE MAPS REF:
53.48548, -9.45515

Portumna

⑮⑨ TRÁ SÁILÍN

COUNTY GALWAY

From Galway city, the coast road through Salthill and Barna runs alongside a string of beaches, some popular and some hardly known. The main beaches each have good car parking but can be busy during the summer season. Take the time to explore one of the many single-track lanes off the shore road to find your own private beach. One such cove is Trá Sáilín – Salty Beach – the perfect spot to pitch your tent on the grass and take a quiet moonlight dip.

Swim from the tiny beach, turning left around the rocky outcrop into the brackish mix where a stream meets the salt water of the bay. As you swim, look due south across the bay to the Burren in County Clare and west to the Aran Islands, hazy in the morning light.

The small beach affords a pleasant dip, shallow as you walk out and hemmed in on each side by the rocks reaching out into Galway Bay. After your swim, take a walk along the shore to warm up.

It is said that September is a particularly good month to swim in the sea as it is then that the seaweeds release their nutrients, reputedly very good for the skin. Sáilín is well known as a good spot for collecting seaweed at that time of the year.

Sáilín cove is a place of quiet solitude where calmness pervades the air. To the left of the beach, between the stream and the beach, is a small, bracken-covered hillock, fenced around. This is protected ground, a graveyard for children who died in the Great Famine between 1845 and 1852. Locals still pay respect to their memory.

Other nearby beaches include Furbogh, An Spidéal and Loughanbeg, all of which are popular, but popular in Ireland is not the busy south of France, littered with folks working on their tans. Ireland's popular beaches always have plenty of room for swimmers and sun worshippers alike.

GALWAY

RIGHT Trá Sáilín

AT A GLANCE

(159) TRÁ SÁILÍN

Wild camping at this tiny, private cove. Swim in the brackish river around to the beach looking out across Galway Bay towards County Clare and the Aran Islands.

BY CAR: 26 minutes from Galway city (or 1 hour 5 minutes by bicycle): take R336 west from Galway city, through Barna and An Spidéal. Look for the small brown signpost 'Trá Sáilín', pointing to the single-track lane that leads to a small turning circle with parking room for four cars. Pitch on the grass above high water and take a late evening or early morning dip.

SKINNY-DIPPING • SECLUDED • WILD CAMPING • BEACH FISHING

GRID REF: M 10266 21973
GOOGLE MAPS REF:
53.24034, -9.34521

(160) SILVERSTRAND

A little farther out along the coast road from Salthill, you will pass several beaches. Silverstrand at Barna is only 6km from Galway city and is a shallow sandy bay suitable for young families. With its promenade and good parking, it affords great views of the stunning Galway Bay. The 250m-long beach is flanked by rocks on one side and a cliff on the other. At low tide, there is a good stretch of sand, yet at high tide the beach is fully covered. Lifeguarded during the summer months.

BY CAR: 7 minutes from Blackrock Diving Tower. Continue west on R336 for 1.2km, turn left to stay on R336/Barna Road for 1.5km. Turn left onto L5148, signed Silverstrand.

BLUE FLAG BEACH • FAMILY FRIENDLY • POPULAR • LIFEGUARDED IN SUMMER

GRID REF: M 24834 22876
GOOGLE MAPS REF:
53.25124, -9.12690

(161) LOUGH REA

Ample amenities make The Long Point the perfect family outing, only 1.2km from Loughrea town. A Blue Flag winner, it has both a small beach to wade in from, and a jetty to jump from. It is ideal for all levels of swimmer. The water is crystal clear with a sand and stone base. Between the two jetties, it gets deep quickly. There's a wooden diving platform at the end of the far jetty. Along the near wall and inside this jetty is a newly installed bar, perfect for the swimmer to hold on to and take a rest. Close to the roadside, the grass area has picnic tables and seating and, from the promenade walkway, there are wide steps into the shallow water.

BY CAR: 1 hour 5 minutes from Galway city. Take R338/Old Dublin Road onto N67 for 9.5km. Exit onto R446 and continue for 26km into Loughrea. Turn left onto Barrack Street, then right onto R351. Continue out of town along the shore for 1.5km to the parking area. Height restrictions on car park.

FAMILY FRIENDLY • LIFEGUARDED IN SUMMER • CHANGING ROOMS WITH SHOWERS

GRID REF: M 62547 15207
GOOGLE MAPS REF:
53.18617, -8.56086

Trá Sáilín

162 TRÁ AN DÓILÍN (THE CORAL BEACH)

COUNTY GALWAY

At the mouth of Galway Bay, wedged between Casla Bay and Greatman's Bay, lies one of the most extraordinary beaches in Ireland: Carrowroe's Coral Beach, or Trá an Dóilín. This unusual beach is made not of sand but of what look like tiny pieces of coral in myriad colours. Scoop a handful and it gleams with the mother-of-pearl of tiny snail shells, minute cornet shells and minuscule pieces of coral, the colours ranging from purple to orange and yellow, and fading to pure sun-bleached white.

At the mouth of Galway Bay is a series of islands, some joined by causeways to the mainland. There are several almost deserted beaches to be found by following the winding roads down to old disused turf quays. Trá an Dóilín has a special appeal and is one not to miss.

This series of small coves nestled between rocky outcrops is filled with coralline algae known as maerl. The tiny branches of delicate underwater plants mingle with hair-fine algae, rich in purple and red hues, all heaped together in their millions, along with the most minute seashells you could hope to find, creating this fascinating beach.

Tread carefully as you explore the rock pools and coves because maerl, while beautiful, is sharp on bare feet. It crunches beneath you as you walk. As you swim in the clear water, those myriad colours beneath catch the light.

Each little cove is sheltered and perfect for swimming, the rocks on either side reaching out and protecting the tiny bays from any strong currents. You can happily make your way along the coast by swimming from one cove to the next. The water is clear and shelves fairly quickly.

Here, too, you may be lucky enough to see a Galway Hooker, the native Irish boat topped with its distinctive dark red sail. Spend an afternoon here rock-pooling and beachcombing (remember to bring your beach shoes).

Although the first bay you come to is overlooked by the car park, there are plenty more small coves and beaches between the rocky outcrops where you can find a secluded spot to swim.

164
163
165

GALWAY

162

ABOVE: Trá an Doilín
LEFT: Maerl

AT A GLANCE

⑯ TRÁ AN DÓILÍN

Carrowroe's Coral Beach is made entirely of coralline algae, of vibrant colours ranging from bleached white to deep purple. The August bank holiday sees the Féile an Dóilín, a Galway Hooker festival in Ireland. Trá an Dóilín has plenty of rock pools, and nooks and crannies to get away from the crowds. Several small coves between rocky outcrops provide quiet swimming. Sandals are recommended as the tiny pieces of maerl can be sharp on sensitive feet.

BY CAR: 55 minutes from Galway city. Take R336 coast road west past Connemara Airport. At Casla/Costelloe, turn left onto R343 and follow the signs for Carrowroe/ An Ceathrú Rua. Drive through the village and look for the signpost for Trá an Dóilín which brings you to the car park and beach.

SNORKELLING • ROCK POOLS • POPULAR • TOILET FACILITIES

GRID REF: L 91301 22996
GOOGLE MAPS REF:
53.24956, -9.63035

⑯ OMEY ISLAND

To walk or drive onto this tidal island, you need to wait for low water. As the tide recedes, signposts emerge from the water like magic, marking the safe route across the hard sand flats onto the island. Following the road to the left, you first come to Omey South Beach, approx. 800m. Steeply shelving, this is best left to strong swimmers. This is a conservation area for dolphins – you may spot some. Continue along the road westwards almost 1km to Omey Beach, which shelves more gently. Above is St Feichin's holy well and you can continue along trails to complete a full loop of the island, 8km in total. **Remember: you can return across the strand only at mid to low tide so check times!**

BY CAR: 18 minutes from Clifden. Take N59 for 3.5km. Turn left onto L1102, signed Claddaghduff. Continue for 8km, passing Clifden Eco Campsite into Claddaghduff. Turn left at Our Lady Star of the Sea Church and continue 750m down to the small car park at the strand. You can leave the car here and walk to Omey or drive across, but remember you can only cross at low tide.

TIDAL ISLAND • TRAIL WALK TO BEACHES • DOLPHINS

GRID REF: L 57883 56440
GOOGLE MAPS REF:
53.53897, -10.14495

⑯ SELERNA BEACH

A stone's throw from Cleggan Pier, where the ferry for Inishbofin leaves, is the idyllic Selerna Beach. Fine white sand shelves quickly into the blue-green Atlantic waters; the rocks on either side of the bay offer some protection. Look for the passing ferry on its way to Inishbofin or farther north to Inishturk.

On the headland to the right of the beach is Knockbrack tomb. A large capstone perches precariously on top of a series of smaller stones, creating a 4m-long chamber. Given the name 'Druids Altar' during the Celtic Revival, it is thought that this was both for burying the dead and for religious ceremonies. The markings on the capstone may have been carved to channel blood towards the ground ...

While here, take the ferry to Inishbofin, and don't forget your swimsuit for its lovely beach too.

BY CAR: 16 minutes from Clifden. Take N59 north for 5.5km. Veer left onto R379/Cleggan/ Inishbofin. Continue past Cleggan Pier and then turn right to the beach.

FAMILY FRIENDLY • WHITE SAND

GRID REF: L 58772 58498
GOOGLE MAPS REF:
53.55765, -10.13323

(165) FOUNTAIN HILL BEACH

Tucked away from the main roads and off down a sandy lane, you can get away from any crowds here. This is a place to leave the car behind and walk or cycle to. Best to park at Omey Strand, from where it's a 30-minute walk along country roads. The west-facing bay is sheltered by Omey Island's southern tip, and at high tide the water gets deep quickly.

BY CAR to Omey Strand: 18 minutes from Clifden, take N59 for 3.5km. Turn left onto L1102, signed Claddaghduff. Continue for 8km, passing Clifden Eco Campsite into Claddaghduff. Turn left at Our Lady Star of the Sea Church for the quay.

From the strand parking area: 30 minutes on foot. Walk approx. 150m south along the beach to an old road. Follow this away from the coast for 800m to join the Claddaghduff Road. Veer right and continue for 600m. Turn right, T road sign, and continue for almost 1km along this single-track road. At the thatched cottage, a sandy laneway leads down towards the beach.

WALKING • SECLUDED

GRID REF: L 58201 55372
GOOGLE MAPS REF:
53.52943, -10.13799

Omey Island

Fountain Hill Beach

⑯ DOG'S BAY AND GURTEEN BEACH

COUNTY GALWAY

In the pretty village of Roundstone, art galleries and studios for handmade ceramics and jewellery vie for space. A walk through the town will bring you to craft shops and there is a good variety of bars, restaurants and cafés which serve locally caught seafood.

The road signs from Roundstone will bring you past Dog's Bay caravan park and then down a lane to a parking area at the first of four beaches, on the west of the tombolo tying an island to the mainland. This is Dog's Bay, a smooth horseshoe beach backed by a grass bank where cattle wander freely.

Taking a clockwise tour from Dog's Bay, cross the narrow spit of land to Gurteen's long and sweeping bay. Gurteen is almost a kilometre long with a caravan park at its north-east end.

Both of these beaches are ideal for swimming. If the wind is too strong at Dog's Bay, it is likely that Gurteen will be sheltered. However, this is not all the area has to offer. Continue clockwise from the southern end of Gurteen and walk west approx. 300m over the delicate grasslands, made up of rare machair vegetation, a habitat found on the west coasts of Ireland and Scotland, to the quiet third beach. The same fine white sand can be found on this raw and exposed beach, where the wind has eaten away the edge of the dunes and the ancient fencing has fallen. Few people walk this far past the docile cattle, yet the reward is a pretty strand all to yourself. Set between two banks of rock and facing almost due south, this small strand is a super swim. To the right of the bay the rocks hide a deep narrow inlet.

From here continue your loop walk north north west for another 400m to the fourth and final treat of the day, a narrow, almost hidden gully with a steep bank of soft sand gouged into the high grass banks.

As you swim out around the rocks to the east of this little cove, you can see the horseshoe strand of Dog's Bay, where you began your walk. It is a mere 240m walk east over the rise from this narrow cove back to Dog's Bay Beach.

167 168

169 166

GALWAY

RIGHT Dog's Bay

AT A GLANCE

166 DOG'S BAY AND GURTEEN BEACH

From an inauspicious start point, the beaches of Dog's Bay and Gurteen are glorious, with fine, pure white sand, lying back to back with just a narrow spit of grassland between them. Discover two more hidden beaches across the bulbous nose of this tied island.

BY CAR: 1 hour 30 minutes from Galway city. Take N59 north west, turning left onto R341 to Roundstone. Follow the signs to Dog's Bay Caravan Park. Continue past the caravan park to a rough track leading to a parking area (at the time of writing, work was ongoing here, with new gravel being laid beside the old and rusty fencing).

BY BUS: Bus Éireann's Clifden-to-Galway route serves Roundstone daily during summer and three days a week in the winter. Dog's Bay is 4km from the town.

SCENIC WALK • FAMILY FRIENDLY • SECLUDED

GRID REF: L 69375 38626
GOOGLE MAPS REF:
53.38094, -9.96325

167 RENVYLE BEACH

Travelling deeper into the heart of Connemara, you pass through bogland and mountains, dotted with loughs and tiny fishing huts, whitewashed miniature cottages in the wild landscape. In the Twelve Pins mountain range, each corner you turn brings a new and exquisite view. At Renvyle, known as Islands View, almost 600m of white strand borders the pure Atlantic water, with superb views out to Inishturk and the nearer and fabulously named Shanvallybeg and Crump Islands. A story goes that when deciding the sea border between Galway and Mayo, the decision was to empty a sack of oats into the sea and wherever the oats landed would mark the border. As they floated, the islands to the north were deemed to be Mayo and those to the south would be Galway.

BY CAR: 1 hour 55 minutes from Galway. Take N59 for 58km. Turn right onto R344 and continue for 5km, then left onto N59 for 6km. Turn right and continue for 7km and then right onto Tully Beg to the small parking area at the beach.

FAMILY FRIENDLY • POPULAR STRAND

GRID REF: L 68602 63700
GOOGLE MAPS REF:
53.60708, -9.98835

168 GURTEEN PIER AND BEACH

Gurteen Pier offers the option of the shallow waters within the pier walls, where a large rock reef creates a sheltered area, or jumping off the end of the pier, at high water. As always with pier jumping, check the depth and that the water is clear. **Rocks to the left of the pier mean no jumping here.** Across these rocks is a small beach. At 200m long, it is a lovely stretch if you prefer doing laps. As with most of the area's beaches, it has that fine sand and crystal-clear waters. Getting quickly to a good swimming depth and fairly sheltered, the beach faces north east towards the mouth of Killary Harbour. At times a mobile sauna pitches here, so there's a chance to warm up after your swim.

BY CAR: 25 minutes from Clifden. Take N59 to Letterfrack. After 14km, turn left onto L1101/Connemara Loop for 5.5km. At Tully, turn right at the petrol station and continue for 1km to the pier.

PIER JUMPING WITH BEACH CLOSE • PARKING

GRID REF: L 69401 63216
GOOGLE MAPS REF:
53.60258, -9.97338

Gurteen Pier and Beach

(169) BALLYCONNEELY BAY BEACH AND MANNIN BAY BLUEWAY

Turquoise-blue waters meet white sand and maerl beaches on this string of beaches that make up the Blueway, a network of trails for kayaking, snorkelling and getting close to sea life. With shallow waters, you can spend a day here moving from one beach to the next, exploring little coves and rock pools. Ballyconneely Beach has a broad, white strand and shallow waters. Connemara is famous for its ponies and its love of racing so you may catch sight of some of Ballyconneely's Connemara ponies.

The breed is believed to have originated when Arabian horses swam ashore from a Spanish shipwreck near Slyne Head and bred with the small native pony.

BY CAR: 11 minutes from Clifden. Take R341 south to Derrygimla. A large lay-by provides ample parking at Mannin Bay. For Ballyconneely beach, park here and walk 450m further along the road, directly opposite the house on the left is a laneway down to the beach. Best at mid to low tide when the sand is exposed. No parking or turning down this lane.

FAMILY FRIENDLY • ROCK POOLS

GRID REF: L 62194 45278
GOOGLE MAPS REF:
53.43919, -10.07427

⑰⓪ GLASSILLAUN

COUNTY GALWAY

Connemara has its own raw beauty – lake-dotted peat bogs and myriad beaches made from stone, shell and fine white sand – and as you travel towards Killary Harbour, the mountains soar up in rugged green banks from the roadside, making you want to jump out of the car and stride into the hills, despite driving rain. The narrow, winding roads weave through the landscape past tiny fisherman's huts, some looking like miniature whitewashed stone cottages. Near the mouth of the deep glacial fjord of Killary Harbour is the pretty Glassillaun Beach.

Breathtaking, even on a grey and windy rainswept day, Glassillaun on the Atlantic coast does not disappoint.

The soft, pale, golden sand sweeps around in a gentle arc from the sand dunes towards a small island to the left of the bay, with its own small beach which mirrors the main strand. On a warm and sunny day, swim from here across to that beach and lie in the sunshine, walk on the grass-topped island and look out across the Atlantic. Bring a picnic and while away the day. At low tide, it is possible to walk across the wet sands out to the island, but remember, the tide will flood in again and you might have to swim to return!

If you have plenty of time, carry on around the headland to the left, past the island, and scramble along the shore to several more secluded coves. **Keep an eye on the tides** for swimming or wading back.

To the right of the main strand, the snorkelling is particularly good around the rocks in the deep channel. Towards Little Killary Bay and Salrock, just north of this channel, beyond a narrow spit of land is Killary Harbour glacial fjord. At 16km long and over 45m deep, it is one of three fjords in Ireland (Belfast and Carlingford Loughs being the others). Killary is known for its seafood so, on your return trip, call at one of the roadside stands for fresh mussels.

MAYO

⑰①⑰② ⑰③⑰⓪

GALWAY

RIGHT Glassillaun

AT A GLANCE

170 GLASSILLAUN

From Glassillaun beach, swim across the beautiful bay to a tiny island with its mini-beach, snorkel east, west and north into Little Killary Bay or at low tide explore the hidden coves around the headland.

BY CAR: 40 minutes from Clifden. Take N59 toward Westport. Pass through Kylemore and then turn left, signposted Renvyle. Continue for 4.5 km. At Tullycross turn right then left following Wild Atlantic Way signs, continue for 6.5km. Turn left, signposted Glassillaun Beach. Continue 1km to the beach parking.

FAMILY FRIENDLY • SCENIC WALK • SNORKELLING

GRID REF: L 75913 64486
GOOGLE MAPS REF:
53.61483, -9.87572

171 CARROWMORE BEACH

The machair grasslands and dunes backing this lovely beach are full of wildlife, plants, insects and birds. This 800m stretch of golden sands from the Bunowen River to Carrowmore Quay is on the shores of Clew Bay, looking across the bay to Achill Island and left, to Clare Island, almost 9km away. Set near the mouth of this square-shaped bay, Carrowmore has little shelter when the waves pick up, but still is a beautiful swim. The pier at the west end of the beach is built along the natural hook of the rocks and provides a sheltered nook from mid to high tide. At low tide, the sand stretches almost to the end of the pier wall.

BY CAR: 25 minutes from Westport. Take N59 south west. Turn right onto R335 and continue for 20km to Louisburgh. Go through the town and turn right. After 1km, turn right again. It is 800m to the beach.

LIFEGUARDED IN THE SUMMER •POPULAR • FAMILY FRIENDLY

GRID REF: L 79710 81521
GOOGLE MAPS REF:
53.77016, -9.82324

172 OLDHEAD BEACH

Oldhead, near Louisburgh, is one of the more popular beaches in Mayo, but it is still a great spot. Swimmers of all levels congregate here, so if it's distance training you want or a relaxing swim with friends, you have a choice. On the southern shores of Clew Bay, the beach draws a variety of users: families, swimmers and surfers, there's space for all. Walkers may want to scale nearby Croagh Patrick, Ireland's holy mountain. On Reek Sunday, the last Sunday in July, thousands walk the path in pilgrimage, and the tradition was to do so barefoot. A good hike with steep sections and some difficulty at the top with loose stones, ensure you are fit and prepared for a long hike.

BY CAR: 21 minutes from Westport. Take N59 south for 1km. Turn right onto R335 and continue for 16.5km. Turn right onto Oldhead Holiday Village and right again to beach parking.

SWIMMING, SURFING AND WATER SPORTS • FAMILY FRIENDLY • POPULAR

GRID REF: L 83424 82205
GOOGLE MAPS REF:
53.64973, -9.88229

Oldhead Beach

(173) SILVER STRAND

A common name but an uncommonly beautiful beach, Silver Strand is remote and near the mouth of Killary Harbour, but it's surprisingly easy to get here. On hot summer days, you may have to share, but come out of season and you are very likely to claim this beach all to yourself. The beach is in a deep inlet with a swathe of sand, sheltered by sand dunes to one side and the Lost Valley and famine village to the other. Behind, the low slopes that lead up towards Mweelrea, the highest mountain in Connacht, make this a wild and beautiful swim.

BY CAR: 45 minutes from Westport. Take N59 and then R335 west for 21km. At Louisburgh, continue onto R378 for 16km. Large car park above the beach.

FAMILY FRIENDLY • PARKING • SCENIC

GRID REF: L 75674 68301
GOOGLE MAPS REF: 53.64973, -9.88229

⑰ KEEM, ACHILL ISLAND

COUNTY MAYO

A visit to Achill Island on the west coast of County Mayo takes you a step back in time to idyllic childhood summers where all day was spent on the beach and treats were an ice cream 'poke' and a fish-and-chip supper. One of the most beautiful beaches on Achill is the picturesque Keem Beach at the western end of the island. The first view of the beach is from the vertiginous road that winds up from Dooagh. This horseshoe bay, set in a steep amphitheatre under Benmore cliffs, is said to have been blessed by St Patrick. With the sun lighting up the deep water, the colours range from a bright turquoise darkening to teal against the vibrant bright green grass on the slopes of Benmore.

Although a popular beach, Keem is never crowded, even at the height of the tourist season. Go down the steep, winding road to the beach and find a quiet spot. Swim around the rocks to the left of the beach where, at low tide, several secluded, sandy coves are revealed. Walkers will enjoy the climb up Croaghaun behind the beach, which affords more spectacular views, before heading west to the cliffs of Benmore.

Looking down to the beach, think of the challenges the local fishermen used to face. It was from this strand that they would set out in their curraghs, the traditional canvas-covered boats used up until the 1940s and 1950s, in search of basking sharks. The oil of the basking shark was an important source of income for the islanders.

Crossing onto the island, which is separated from the mainland by a single bridge, the road onto Achill goes through the peat bog landscape towards the village of Keel. The roads taper and black-faced sheep wander unconcerned along the tarmac. These narrow roads and unhurried atmosphere make the island well suited to cycling trips. The campsite at Keel is well equipped, although it can be busy in the summer. Surfing is popular here and the long strand is a moment's walk from the campsite.

Take a bicycle or car and travel around the island, visit the Deserted Village at Slievemore and walk in the hills.

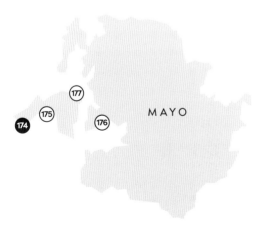

MAYO

Keem Beach

AT A GLANCE

174 KEEM, ACHILL ISLAND

Swim where fishermen launched their curraghs in search of basking sharks. Follow the main Achill Road, R319, through Dooagh village, climbing above the coast for spectacular views down to Keem. The left-hand side of the beach is quieter. Walk up the ridge onto Croaghaun Mountain and enjoy the spectacular views from the Benmore Cliffs.

BY CAR: 1 hour 7 minutes from Westport. Take N59 for 29km, through Mulranny. Turn left onto R319, which takes you across Achill, through Keel and Dooagh, and leads directly to Keem Bay, ending at a car park above the beach.

POPULAR • FAMILY FRIENDLY • SNORKELLING

GRID REF: F 56126 04323
GOOGLE MAPS REF:
53.96752, -10.19348

175 KEEL BEACH

This large beach is popular with swimmers and surfers, and the waves crashing in are exhilarating. At 3km in length, you can roam the beach and play in the surf. **Avoid the eastern end of the beach, which is notorious for strong currents.** During the summer, there are designated swim areas, which are lifeguarded, and surf schools for those who want to try out surfing. The campsite behind the beach is a super place to base yourself for exploring the rest of Achill, on foot, two wheels or four, whatever your preference.

BY CAR: 56 minutes from Westport. Take N59 for 29km through Mulranny. Turn left onto R319. Stay on R319 for 14km, passing the golf club and then turn left onto Keel Holiday Cottages and down to the beach.

FAMILY FRIENDLY • SURFING, SWIMMING • LIFEGUARDED IN SUMMER • TOILETS, PARKING AND CAMPSITE

GRID REF: F 64745 04356
GOOGLE MAPS REF:
53.97169, -10.07154

176 MULRANNY BEACH

These storm beaches are formed by rocks thrown up by the high storm waters then left behind to create a barrier protecting the delicate saltmarshes behind. Best to swim at mid to low tide as that is when the hard sand is revealed and you have easy access into the gently shelving bay. After your swim, take a walk along the causeway, crossing onto the saltmarsh via the Victorian-style bridge. In springtime, flowers bloom among the system of channels, sand, sea and machair grassland. Finally you will come to the tree-lined path and steps leading up to the Mulranny Park Hotel.

BY CAR: 30 minutes from Westport. Take N59 for 29km to Mulranny. Turn left onto L1404, signed Trá and Spanish Armada. Another left, at the fork, brings you to the beach parking.

FAMILY FRIENDLY • POPULAR • CAUSEWAY WALK

GRID REF: L 82740 95709
GOOGLE MAPS REF:
53.89759, -9.78431

(177) DOONIVER BEACH

Located on the east coast of Achill, close to the Bulls Mouth, only 530m from Inishbiggle, Dooniver is a beautiful sandy bay. With 750m of golden sands, sheltered from the wild Atlantic, it makes for perfect swimming and family days on the beach. At the height of summer, you may find it a bit busy but, as Achill is blessed with many beautiful beaches, there is always room to find your space. For an active trip, bring your bike and range the island at a slower pace. Don't forget your hiking boots for the hills in the west.

BY CAR: 1 hour from Westport. Take N59 for 29 km through Mulranny. Turn left onto R319. Continue for 20km onto Achill to Bunacurry. Turn right onto L1406. After 2.5km, turn right and then, after 0.5km, turn left. Continue for 1.5km down to beach. Limited parking on the grass bank above the beach.

**FAMILY FRIENDLY •
SHELTERED BAY**

GRID REF: F 72879 07613
GOOGLE MAPS REF:
54.00291, -9.93983

Keel Beach

Dooniver Beach

178 + 179 LOUGH NAKEEROGE AND ANNAGH STRAND

COUNTY MAYO

Lough Nakeeroge is the lowest corrie lake in Ireland, just 16m above sea level and separated from the sea by a narrow bridge of grass and heather. Close by are the remains of a booley village (occupied for part of the year, usually to allow livestock to graze on fresh pastures), including a beehive-shaped stone building at the western end of the strand.

Following the cycle loop from Keel, turn right at the Minaun Bar for the road inland to the Deserted Village. This site dates back to the Neolithic period, some 5,000 years ago. The remains we now see are of the village abandoned during the Great Famine in 1845.

To find the gorgeous Nakeeroge and Annagh Bay, park at the graveyard, follow the track past the village and on towards the quarry, where quartz stone blazes white on the path on a sunny day against the green and purple heather.

From the quarry, continue uphill on the rough track towards Slievemore signal tower, for wonderful views across the island looking back towards Keel. Continue over the next rise, keeping Slievemore to your back. At the top you are rewarded with your first view of Lough Nakeeroge and Annagh Strand. There are no roads here: the only way in or out is to walk or travel by boat. After a long walk on a hot day, the lough is a beautiful freshwater swim, right next to the sea. **Remember to give yourself time before darkness falls for the steep climb back to the Deserted Village, a good hour's walk. Keep an eye on the weather conditions, too,** because mist can drop down quickly from Slievemore.

If you have less time, the eastern end of Annagh Bay is a shorter walk: from the quarry, veer right and continue over the low ridge between Slievemore and the signal tower. As the shore comes into view, there is a craggy cove to the right. Several inlets cut into the rocks here are great for jumping. Scramble over the rocks into deep water and explore the coastline, where cormorants fish and seagulls wheel overhead. **This is an adventure swim for the strong swimmer and care should be taken to swim only in calm conditions.**

182

179   180   181

178

MAYO

Lough Nakeeroge

AT A GLANCE

178 LOUGH NAKEEROGE

Lough Nakeeroge: a mountain walk to swim in a freshwater lough mere metres from the Atlantic waters.

BY CAR: 11 minutes from Keel plus an hour's walk. Drive from Keel on R319, turn right at the Minaun Bar onto the Slievemore Road and follow the signs to the Deserted Village. Park here. It is an hour's walk to the lough. Follow the rough track up through the quarry towards the signal tower on the hill above. Continue over the next mountain from which the first view of Lough Nakeeroge appears. No road access.

ADVENTURE SWIM • SCENIC WALK • BEACH CAMPING • DIFFICULT PATH • SECLUDED • REMOTE

GRID REF: F 59995 07476
GOOGLE MAPS REF:
53.99798, –10.13703

179 ANNAGH STRAND

Walk through heather and quartz in this bogland to a rocky cove for an adventure swim with jumping. Swim only in calm conditions. Strong swimmers only. There are many tales of ghostly apparitions at Annagh so those of a superstitious nature should avoid camping here!

BY CAR: As above to the Deserted Village. Park here and follow the track past the village to the quarry. Veer right and continue over the ridge with Slievemore on your right and the signal tower on your left. It is a 40-minute walk from the Deserted Village; no road access.

SCENIC WALK • SNORKELLING • SECLUDED • REMOTE • JUMPING WITH CARE • ROCKS AND HAZARDS • DIFFICULT PATH • ADVENTURE SWIM

GRID REF: F 62362 07787
GOOGLE MAPS REF:
54.00110, –10.10006

180 DOOGORT BEACH/ SILVER STRAND

A Special Conservation Area with the rare machair low grassland that is all across Achill, this is still a popular strand. With plenty of holiday accommodation, Silver Strand is likely to be busy at the height of season. Sheltered from the Atlantic winds by Slievemore mountain to the west, you can swim here year round. This is the location for Achill's New Year's Day dip, if you fancy joining the locals for that!

BY CAR: 1 hour from Westport. Take N59 for 29km through Mulranny. Turn left onto R319 and continue for 22km to Achill and through Bunacurry. Turn right onto Keel Holiday Cottages. After 2.5km, turn right onto Slievemore Road. It is 1km to beach parking.

POPULAR, FAMILY-FRIENDLY BEACH • LIFEGUARDED IN SUMMER

GRID REF: F 67297 08792
GOOGLE MAPS REF:
54.01134, –10.02400

Doolough Strand

(182) DOOLOUGH STRAND

This scenic beach is several kilometres long, with stunning views of Achill in the south and Belmullet to the west. The water here is warm and superb for swimming at high tide. Near the seaside village of Gweesalia, Doolough is famed for the annual horse races in August and for being the setting of J.M. Synge's *Playboy of the Western World*. The plot may be based on a story he heard, while staying in Gweesalia, of an Achill man who assaulted his employer, an English lady. Sheltered by the locals, he then disguised himself as a woman and took the boat to Achill to finally escape to America.

BY CAR: 16 minutes from Bangor Erris in west Mayo. Take R313 and then turn left onto L1206. After 11km, turn right onto L1205. Continue for 3km before turning left, signed Trá. Continue for 2km, then turn left at the fork from where it is 1km down to beach. Park on the grass.

At low tide a channel is revealed between Doolough and Dooyork, this is known for quicksand, so do not enter this channel.

SCENIC VIEWS • AUGUST HORSE RACES • BEWARE AREAS OF QUICKSAND AT SOUTHERN END OF BEACH

GRID REF: F 72556 23113
GOOGLE MAPS REF:
54.14136, -9.95119

(181) DOOGORT EAST BEACH/ GOLDEN STRAND

Facing north over to Blacksod on the tip of Belmullet Peninsula, this golden strand is a great family spot. Gently shelving and with low dunes, it is less sheltered from the wind than its sister, Silver Strand. Nonetheless, it is a cracking place for a swim. Do laps of its 650m length and then get a warmer at Mastersons Bar and Anchor Restaurant. The caravan park behind means this is well used in summer but off season, it's a different story.

BY CAR: 1 hour from Westport. Take N59 for 29km through Mulranny. Turn left onto R319 and continue for 20km onto Achill to Bunacurry. Turn right onto L1406 and continue for 4.3km. Turn left and then left again. Continue for 1km, past the caravan park to the parking bay, and walk from here.

POPULAR FAMILY BEACH

GRID REF: F 69561 08905
GOOGLE MAPS REF:
54.01368, -9.99083

⑱ POLLACAPPUL

COUNTY MAYO

This hidden gem is little known, tucked away down a long laneway, and absolutely stunning. As you crest the hill on the rough single-track lane through farmland, look to the right to see the breathtaking vista of this secluded beach. Cross an old concrete stile and a field to a second stile, which leads onto the beach.

The water is clear, shallow and gently shelving; a small cave to the left provides shelter on windy days and, if you swim out around the rocks to the left of the beach, there is a tiny narrow cove, perfect for naked sunbathing.

Sitting here, you will see an arch in front. At low tide, it is possible to walk through. Is this tiny cove a jellyfish nursery? You may see iridescence flashing from the jelly-babies as they catch the sunlight, turning in the gentle tides. Few people venture to this less-popular part of the Mullet Peninsula, and this beach, tucked as it is so far off the beaten track, will probably be completely deserted, leaving you to enjoy the tranquil solitude of this gorgeous bay.

Rather than taking the main road south on the Mullet Peninsula, turn instead north east and take the less-travelled route, away from the majority of tourists, towards Broadhaven Lighthouse. This road winds between rolling hills and just before Ballyglass, look to the left for the small brown sign for Pollacappul. The single-track road goes along the shore to a farm from where there is a stony lane up over the hill. At the top of the hill the beach is revealed, tantalisingly close, just below the fields to the right. Here the track is wide enough to pull a car in to the side and allow any other vehicle to pass (rare though that will be). Park beside the concrete stile and follow the fence down to the beach.

Bring a picnic for this trip as, once you get here, if the weather is good, you will not want to leave. Having this pristine beach all to oneself to swim and sunbathe and laze the day away is bliss!

MAYO

ABOVE AND LEFT
Pollacappul Beach

AT A GLANCE

 **POLLACAPPUL**

A perfect secluded beach to skinny-dip and sunbathe, miles from the tourist crowds. There are rocks to climb along the coast and inlets to explore.

BY CAR: 11 minutes from Belmullet (or 35 minutes by bicycle). Cross the bridge from Belmullet and follow R313, travelling north towards Ballyglass. The road bends sharply right and continues for several kilometres. At the sign for Pollacappul Rock and Beach Fishing, turn left down a single-track road. Continue past the farmhouse where the tarmac runs out; the rough lane goes farther up through the farmland. Pull in close to the fence at the stone stile and walk the track down to the beach.

SECLUDED • SKINNY-DIPPING • SCENIC WALK

GRID REF: F 75088 36615
GOOGLE MAPS REF:
54.26324, -9.91826

184 BELMULLET TIDAL POOL

Open year round, this purpose-built 20m-long sea pool is free to use. Looking out towards Blacksod Bay, on the shores of the narrow land bridge that leads onto Belmullet Peninsula, it's in a perfect location. Split into two sections, there's a small shallow pool for youngsters and a larger pool which slopes from shallow to deep. The perfect place to get your swim hit without filling the car full of sand afterwards! Lifeguarded in the summer and with summer swim lessons, it's a source of local pride that the pool has remained open for many years.

BY CAR: 1 hour 10 minutes from Westport. Take N59 north to Bangor Erris. Turn left onto R313 and continue 18km to Belmullet. Turn left and then right at the first cross street. Turn left onto Ocean View, then left and then right onto Shore Road. There is limited parking opposite the tidal pool.

PERFECT FOR FAMILIES • LIFEGUARDED AND SWIM LESSONS IN SUMMER

GRID REF: F 70255 31648
GOOGLE MAPS REF:
54.21741, -9.99004

185 ELLY BAY BEACH

On the roadside from Belmullet to Blacksod Harbour, the great curve of Elly Bay calls out for you to stop and drink in the views back across to mainland Mayo. Facing east, this bay is sheltered, and the gently shelving white sands make it the ideal stop-off after a long drive. A Blue Flag beach set in this deep natural curve in the shoreline makes it perfect for a swim to cool down and refresh your spirit before exploring the rest of the peninsula. At this point, the peninsula narrows to less than 300m between the west and east shores and the narrow spit is broken only by sand dunes and the road you are on. On the western shore, the more exposed strand stretches 1.5km and makes for a bracing waterside walk.

BY CAR: 13 minutes from Belmullet. Take R313 for 11.7km. The road runs right along the beach.

BLUE FLAG BEACH • FAMILY FRIENDLY • SWIMMING, SURFING AND WATERSPORTS

GRID REF: F 63723 25693
GOOGLE MAPS REF:
54.16230, -10.08676

(186) GLOSH BAY BEACH

This quiet beach is beautiful to walk along searching for flotsam, and strong swimmers will enjoy the Atlantic waves, which are large enough to bodysurf and bodyboard. Replete with fine white sand, this southern section of beach is 500m long and looks out to the Inishkea islands.

A small rock outcrop separates it from the next beach on this stretch of coastline. Walking north along the sands and across each small rock outcrop, you can travel 3.5km to Tiraun Point. Take the lane down to the Gaelic pitch and then walk the last few metres onto this lovely beach.

BY CAR: 20 minutes from Belmullet. Follow R313 for 17km to Aghleam. Turn right onto L5231. Continue for 1.3km and then turn right down towards beach. Limited parking along this track (ensure you don't block gates or access).

BODYBOARDING AND BODYSURFING • STRONG CURRENTS

GRID REF: F 61290 20175
GOOGLE MAPS REF:
54.11187, -10.12236

Belmullet Tidal Pool

Glosh Bay beach

⓵⑧⑦ PORTACLOY

COUNTY MAYO

**Off the main R314 route from Belderg
to Belmullet, and hidden between
Port Durlainne and Carrowteige,
the sheltered white-sand beach of
Portacloy lies in a natural harbour. Safe
from the Atlantic swell, it is the perfect
place to camp, enjoy swims across the
bay or take the scenic walk over the
headland to Carrowteige.**

Portacloy's Green Coast beach sits virtually
empty, with white cottages dotting the hillside.
A large stone on the roadside is handsomely
engraved, welcoming visitors to the cove. And
that is all there is: no shop, no streets, just a
winding road leading to a short, sandy lane
onto the beach.

Park on the lane beside a small football field
which houses a portacabin. As you walk onto
the stunning beach, you wonder why no one
else is here. The water is clear, the sand soft and
white, shelving gradually, which makes it ideal
for all levels of swimmer.

To the left/western side of the bay, there is an
old slipway and pier where you can jump into
deeper water. From the pier, trail markers guide
you on a loop walk along the cliffs which link
to Carrowteige on the far side of the headland.
The full loop walk of Benwee Head, taking in
the Children of Lir sculpture, is 10km.

This is the perfect place to while away a few
days, swimming and exploring the cove, hours
of scrambling over the rocks and plunging into
the narrow inlet.

Carrowteige Beach and sand dunes are another
great place to camp: it is possible to drive up to
the low dune system, where little grass-topped,
sandy hummocks create a maze of pitching
spots, sheltered from the wind and prying
eyes. Take the time to do one of the four loop
walks from Carrowteige. The trailhead is at
Carrowteige Summer School beside Garvin's
grocery and hardware store. These cliff-edge
trails give great views over Broadhaven Bay's
rocky islands. The Children of Lir Loop is
10km, the Black Ditch Loop is 13km and the
Carrowteige Beach Loop is 6.5km.

MAYO

RIGHT Portacloy

AT A GLANCE

187 PORTACLOY

A gem of a place with everything: a beach, rocky crags, wild camping, jumping and headland walk. From the pier at Portacloy, the Carrowteige Loop Walk goes over the headland and, on the approach, a mere 100m from the second pier, is the inlet.

BY CAR: 1 hour 10 minutes from Ballina. Head north west along R314, through Killala, Ballycastle and Belderg. The road then drops away from the coast until coming to a right turn towards Ceathrú Thaidhg (Carrowteige). Follow the signs for Ceathrú Thaidhg Loop, turn right onto a narrow road and soon pass a rock on roadside inscribed Portacloy. Go straight down this road, around a sharp left-hand bend. A short sandy track leads to the beach. There is limited parking in the laneway.

SCENIC WALK • FAMILY FRIENDLY • BEACH CAMPING • JUMPING WITH CARE

GRID REF: F 84064 43969
GOOGLE MAPS REF:
54.33136, -9.78317

188 BALLYCASTLE BEACH

A little away from the very popular Ross Strand at Killala, Ballycastle Beach is a somewhat quieter choice. In summer, there may be a few campers on the green above the beach. Teased by the caption 'look out for the mermaid's fin', you'll need to be here at low water to see it. At first glance, from the high point of the car park, you might think it refers to the shape of the strand, with the incoming waves creating a series of curves resembling a fluted tailfin, and a stream cutting through the centre of the strand a spine. But then, as the tide retreats, to the right of the stream, a shadow of rocks and dark sand begins to reveal the long, thin tail and the wider fluke as if etched in the sand. The tail is claimed to be that of the little mermaid Erin.

BY CAR: 30 minutes from Ballina. Take R314 through Killala to Ballycastle. Drive through Ballycastle and you'll see a sign on the left to Nephin. On the right is a Trá sign: drive down this road to the shore where there is a mid-sized parking area.

POPULAR • FAMILY FRIENDLY

GRID REF: G 10189 39411
GOOGLE MAPS REF:
54.29610, -9.37745

189 BELDERG HARBOUR AND TIDAL POOL

Continue along the road from Ballycastle past some stunning views of Downpatrick Head and its iconic sea stack. In front, on the hills, you will see the intriguing glisten of the glazed pyramid that marks the Céide Fields. If you have time, check out these ancient field systems, the oldest known in the world. The walls, tombs and dwelling places preserved under the bogland date back to 3700 BC and were discovered in the 1930s by a local teacher cutting turf.

The quaint harbour is a gem tucked away, and if it's not too busy with fishing boats, there are steps down to a tiny corner of sand beside the slipway where you can get into the water. Don't miss out on the tidal pool, though, just over the pier wall. You'll see steps with a metal railing leading over the wall on the left-hand side. As soon as you reach the top step, the tidal pool is opened to you: a natural rock pool, which has been enhanced by minimal extras, good steps and a small, concreted area for ease of access. Shallow at this near side and getting a little deeper to the far side, it's not deep enough for diving but a great spot for a dip and great for kids. Filled every high tide, there are plenty of small rock pools to search for tiny creatures.

BY CAR: 20 minutes from Ballycastle. Follow the coast road

Belderg Harbour and Tidal Pool

R314 past the Céide Fields to Belderg. Pass the cemetery and St Teresa's church. Take a sharp right, signed Prehistoric Farm, and follow the road down to Belderg Pier. Limited parking. Walk to the pier wall and climb the steps to the tidal pool.

TIDAL ROCK POOL • FAMILY FRIENDLY • PIER JUMPING WITH CARE

GRID REF: F 99047 41293
GOOGLE MAPS REF: 54.31153, -9.55290

190 RINROE BEACH

Tucked in on the right-hand side of the spit of land that juts out from Carrowteige Beach is the sandy Rinroe Beach. With a cave to explore, the Carrowteige looped walks nearby and views across Broadhaven Bay to the lighthouse at Ballyglass in Belmullet, this is a super spot to spend a night. It feels remote and, with no facilities except temporary toilets in the summer, you should come prepared to wild camp. It shelves quickly to deep water so it is best to stay close to shore. Care should be taken swimming close to the cliffs on either side as eddy currents can be created by the tides.

BY CAR: 30 minutes from Bangor Erris. Take R313 west. Turn right onto L1204 for 9.5km and then right onto R314. After 4km, turn left at Glenamoy Bridge onto L1023 for 11km. Turn left and continue through Carrowteige. At the end of this road, turn left, signed to the beach. Park either on the dunes or follow the road to Rinroe viewpoint.

BEACH CAMPING • SECLUDED • SPECTACULAR VIEWS • SNORKELLING • CAVE TO EXPLORE • EDDY CURRENTS • SHELVES STEEPLY

GRID REF: F 79991 40890
GOOGLE MAPS REF: 54.30556, -9.83583

191 ROSS STRAND

A popular Blue Flag beach 5km north of Killala town at the mouth of Killala Bay estuary, Ross Strand is great for swimming, walking and birdwatching, with the mudflats providing rich feeding for wildfowl and waders. The Moy River sweeping to the sea here can create strong currents so swim at the designated zones and resist the temptation to swim across to Bartragh Island. Albeit close, the currents can be very strong here.

BY CAR: 22 minutes from Ballina. Take R314 through Killala. Continue on R314 to a sign pointing right to Ross Strand, from where it's 3km to the beach and car park. There is plenty of car parking and toilet facilities. Check with lifeguards for safe swimming areas and times.

POPULAR • LIFEGUARDED • STRONG CURRENTS

GRID REF: G22928 32756
GOOGLE MAPS REF: 54.23258, -9.19782

⑲² AUGHRIS HEAD

COUNTY SLIGO

Twenty minutes west of Sligo, turn off the main road and travel down the narrow and twisting rural lanes to the thatched Beach Bar in Aughris, which serves superb food. There is a long, stony beach here but the better beach by far is 25 minutes away on the Aughris Head walk.

Birds flit across the grassy path as you stroll along. Brambles line the fence and autumn is a good time for blackberry gathering. The path follows the rocky coastline and looking back towards the Beach Bar affords superb views across Sligo Bay to Benbulben Mountain. After about twenty minutes, the path broadens, and a length of wooden fence leads down to the first of two rocky inlets calling out to be explored.

The second has a stony beach providing easy access to the water. Five minutes farther along, the path again broadens out before sweeping around to the left above a curved black-sand beach. Tiny starfish lie washed up on the shore. From this beach you can swim around the rocky headland on the left into a second cove. Accessible only either by swimming or by boat, this cove feels far removed from the rest of the world. Take care making your way through the narrow gap.

In this second cove, low tide reveals shallow caves under the overhanging rocks to explore. Dive under the low arches to swim under the rock walls from one cave into another – if you're brave enough!

To start the walk, follow the road up from the bar to the crossroads, turn right and walk to the small harbour, where the road sweeps sharply to the left (a sign warns cars of the steep slipway). A bungalow is directly ahead. The walk starts between it and the slipway; the grass path is well mown, and a fence keeps walkers safe from the edge.

The path continues to a holy well, crossing cattle fields. Return by the same path to the Beach Bar, where you can while away the night in the popular pub and even pitch your tent in the garden for a small fee.

ABOVE AND LEFT
Rocky inlets at Aughris
Head

AT A GLANCE

192 AUGHRIS HEAD

A coastal walk then a swim from one cove to the next, finally return to the Beach Bar for a great meal and a pint before settling down for the night, camping in the bar's beachfront garden.

This small campsite has basic facilities, and it can be a little noisy depending on who's in the pub, but it has a very friendly atmosphere.

BY CAR: 40 minutes from Sligo town. Take N4 south for 6.4km. Exit onto N59/Ballina, continue on N59 for 22km. Turn right onto L6205/Laragh, signs also for Beach Bar. After 1.5km, turn left. In 1km turn right (signposted Aughris Head Pier and Beach Bar), continue for 1.5km and turn right down to the Beach Bar and parking.

SCENIC WALK • FAMILY FRIENDLY • SECLUDED • ADVENTURE SWIM • SECOND COVE FOR STRONG SWIMMERS • CAVES • GOOD FOOD • BEACH CAMPING

GRID REF: G 50822 36232
GOOGLE MAPS REF:
54.27265, -8.75561

Sandy Bay

193 SANDY BAY, LOUGH CONN

This bay is not exactly sandy – more that fine silty sand, not quite mud – but on a clear day, it's an appealing spot. Clearly used by those in the know, the area is tucked away from the road and not overlooked by any of the neighbouring houses.

Very shallow, you may find at times of little rain that you can walk out to the little crannog in the bay. There are plenty of trees and bushes with pops of wild flowers attracting dragonflies and butterflies – a nice spot to cool off while exploring the back roads.

BY CAR: 15 minutes from Ballina. Take N26 south, after 3km turn right onto R310/Pontoon, continue for 2.6km. At the junction turn right then immediately left towards Cloghans. Continue for 2.3km. The road sweeps right. In 0.5km at the end of this road turn left onto Friarstown, continue 1.8km, turn right. In 300m veer right, continue 900m, just before the road sweeps sharply to the left is the track to shore. Take care parking after rain as it gets muddy.

GRID REF: G 19541 10907
GOOGLE MAPS REF:
54.0412, -9.22907

(194) LOUGH CULLIN

This series of small sandy beaches invites you to slow down and take in the views. Each has a stony parking area and space for picnicking. The shoreline is shallow, and rocks loom out of the water at all angles. You may have to wade out a fair bit to get depth. But the views are spectacular!

The second beach's parking area is opposite the entrance to Drummin Wood trail, an easy 5km walk. The third and nicest beach is just a little farther along and has a good-sized parking area. Picnic benches set up on either side of a large, flat stone create a novel picnic table. A row of great rocks line the shore.

As with the other beaches, the water is shallow and rocky so take care. Check out Terrybaun Pottery close to Foxford for interesting souvenirs.

BY CAR: 20 minutes from Ballina. Take N26 and then R310 through Knockmore. Follow the shore of Lough Conn. At the junction, swing left to continue on R318/ Foxford. The first of the three sandy beaches is about 1km along this road. Each has limited parking.

FAMILY FRIENDLY • PICNIC AREA • ROCKY AND SHALLOW

GRID REF: G 23962 04435
GOOGLE MAPS REF:
53.98374, -9.16007

(195) AN POLL GORM, EASKY

An Poll Gorm – 'the blue hole' – is a natural swimming hole on the coastal cliffs near Easky. This long, narrow inlet has been a favourite swim spot for decades. In 1967, a containing wall was built by locals to create this tidal pool, making it a safe spot for swimmers. Winter seas took their toll on this wall over the years, and so money was raised. In 2016, the local LEAP Project undertook to rejuvenate it and now, more than fifty years after its initial inception, the pool is back to its former glory. While surfers hit the big waves, swimmers can enjoy the safety of this tidal pool, refilled at each high water.

BY CAR: 40 minutes from Sligo. Take N4 south and then N59/ Ballina, continue for 34km to Dromore West. Turn right onto R297 for 5km, then turn right and continue for 2km towards the coast. Look for the small square in the field for containing sheep – An Poll Gorm is across the rocks opposite.

NATURAL TIDAL ROCK POOL • FAMILY FRIENDLY • NO LIFEGUARDS

GRID REF: G 38647 38658
GOOGLE MAPS REF:
54.29321, -8.94210

(196) ENNISCRONE BEACH

Surfing and swimming mix here on this popular beach. It is a holiday destination and so gets busy in the summer months and has lifeguarded swimming areas. Off season, the beach is still well used so you often meet other swimmers or surfers.

With 5km of sand stretching from Enniscrone across the mouth of the River Moy to Bartragh Island, you can walk across at low tide to roam the strand and dunes. Make sure you leave time to return before the tide.

BY CAR: 50 minutes from Sligo town. Take N4 and then N59 for 39km. Turn right onto R298. After 5km, turn left onto R297 and after 3km turn right onto Bridge Street and follow around to the beach parking.

POPULAR FAMILY BEACH
• BUSY SEASIDE TOWN
• LIFEGUARDED DURING SUMMER

GRID REF: G 28482 29900
GOOGLE MAPS REF:
54.21248, -9.09820

⟨197⟩ BISHOP'S POOL AND MULLAGHMORE BEACH

COUNTY SLIGO

Take a walk, run or cycle along the rugged cliffs of Mullaghmore Head, where the Wild Atlantic Way lives up to its name. The Loop Road goes past a local favourite: Bishop's Pool. At high tide, the Atlantic floods in to create this tidal pool, large enough for swimming and deep enough for jumping and diving. This rock pool brims full of sea life, a perfect nursery with mini-starfish and tiny crabs creeping among the anemones and baby eels, less than an inch long, scooting through the water and leaping out of the way when disturbed.

This is probably the worst-kept 'secret swimming' place because locals and visitors alike flock here at high tide and the place is a hive of activity.

The rock pool bustles with generations of swimmers and divers. The stepped rocks provide hours of scrambling with various heights to jump from into the deep pool. Great swathes of green carpetweed cascade over the black rocks and highlight the ruggedness of the place.

At low tide, there is still the opportunity to do some rock-pooling, hunting for shrimp and minute sea creatures in the shallow pools left behind.

The isolated Classiebawn Castle stands out on the skyline, perched alone on the exposed and barren Mullaghmore Head behind. Mermaids Cove can be seen across the bay on the other side of Mullaghmore town. Its quiet, family-friendly beach, only 20 minutes from the busy surfing Mecca of Bundoran, is a great place to swim, snorkel and bodyboard. It suits its whimsical name as the beach is dotted with rocks and caves which may well hide some of the elusive mythical creatures in the dimming twilight.

Spend an evening out on Mullaghmore Head watching the light change and listening to the crash of the ocean. Feel the ground shake with the immense power of the Atlantic swell as the huge Atlantic rollers, known as prowlers, crash onto Mullaghmore Head. Unsurprisingly, this is one of the best big-wave surfing locations in the world.

Bishop's Pool

AT A GLANCE

197 BISHOP'S POOL AND MULLAGHMORE BEACH

Jump and dive in the Bishop's Pool, with rock-pooling at low tide where you might search for whelks, anemone or tiny crabs. Or visit Mullaghmore beach to swim or surf.

BY CAR: 28 minutes north of Sligo town. Take N15 north to Cliffoney and turn left onto R279. For Bishop's Pool, turn left at T-junction to stay on R279 into Mullaghmore. Take the Loop Road through Mullaghmore, passing the beach parking, keeping to the right around the headland. Stop at the small gravel parking bay with a well-tended grass picnic area and walk down the grassy bank to the large rock pool.

BY BUS: the nearest bus stop is at Cliffoney approximately 5km from Mullaghmore. Bus Éireann operates local and Expressway services. (Check their website for schedules.)

FAMILY FRIENDLY • TIDAL POOL • JUMPING WITH CARE

GRID REF: G 70803 58203
GOOGLE MAPS REF:
54.47262, -8.45536

Streedagh Beach

198 STREEDAGH BEACH

This large strand is exposed to both wind and waves, so swim with caution. However, on a good day, the fine white sand and large, gently shelving bay is glorious. A popular spot with locals, on windy days you may well be sharing the waves with surfers. With 2.5km of beach all the way to Conor's Island, and more coves and sands to explore there, you are sure to find your space. When you arrive at the spacious parking area, you are in the lee of the low sand dunes, so if it's windy here, it will be very windy on the beach behind!

BY CAR: 24 minutes north of Sligo town. Take N15 north for 13km.

Turn left. After 2km, turn right. After 1km, turn left and continue for 2km down to Streedagh beach parking.

SURF AND SWIMMING • LONG STRAND TO WALK • CAUTION NEEDED ON WINDY DAYS

GRID REF: G 63704 50766
GOOGLE MAPS REF:
54.40426, -8.55898

(199) SPENCER HARBOUR

A well-maintained harbour on Lough Allen for small boats, fishing and touring but usually quiet, this spot is ideal for a swim. The large pontoon has a couple of ladders but **check the depth before jumping or diving!** To the right of the pontoon, a metal bench sits on a clipped grass area. You can see a track from here into the water and it's from here you can navigate a path, avoiding the large rocks, and quickly get to swimming depth. Corry Island lies ahead, a sheltered 275m swim out to the near side. **Watch for rocks near the shore.**

BY CAR: 55 minutes from Enniskillen. Take the A4/Sligo Road for 12.2 miles (19.6km) to Blacklion. Continue onto N16 for 2.5 miles (4km), then turn left onto R207 for 8 miles (13km). At Dowra, turn right onto R200 and continue for 6.5 miles (10.5km). Turn left, then right and then left again onto R280 at Breffni Court. After 2 miles (3km), turn left onto the narrow lane leading to the jetty.

QUIET LAKE SWIM • FAMILY FRIENDLY • SWIM TO ISLAND

GRID REF: G 93547 21471
GOOGLE MAPS REF:
54.14137, -8.09907

(200) CORMONGAN PIER

This is one of the most easily accessed swim spots on Lough Allen. It has a small parking area with picnic tables, a slipway to the right and a narrow concrete jetty to the left with a tiny pocket of lake sand between. Off the slipway is pretty stony so use either the sand or the jetty. You can swim on either side of this jetty and get some shelter from the chop created by wind over the water. **Too shallow for diving off the jetty.** While you're in the area non-cold-water swimmers might like to try outdoor swimming in Drumshanbo's heated outdoor pool. Just beside Acres Lake, it's run by Aura Leisure and open during the summer months.

BY CAR: 45 minutes from Enniskillen. Take the A4/Sligo Road to Blacklion, 12.2 miles (19.6km). Continue onto N16 for 2.5 miles (4km), then turn left onto R207 for 15 miles 924km) before turning right and then left, signed for the pier. (Drumshanbo is 3 miles (5km) farther along on R207, heading south.)

EASY ACCESS • HEATED OUTDOOR POOL NEARBY • NO DIVING FROM JETTY

GRID REF: G 97702 15888
GOOGLE MAPS REF:
54.09220, -8.03583

(201) GULLADOO LOUGH

A ribbon lake in Leitrim with one toe in Longford and a very short distance from Cavan, Gulladoo is almost on the convergence of three provinces: Ulster, Leinster and Connacht.

In the middle of its length, the lake is squeezed into a narrow gap only a few metres wide. This pinch point in the lough is where a small single-lane bridge spans the gap. Just before the bridge is a little wooded picnic area with brightly coloured tables and benches, stone steps into the water and space to park about eight cars. A row of tin huts (locked at time of writing) reflect the evening sunlight. It's stony to walk in here but access in and out is easy. Enjoy an evening swim and warm up with hot drinks and a picnic afterwards.

BY CAR: 1 hour 20 minutes from Sligo. Take N4 to Carrick-on-Shannon. Continue on N4 for another 8km, then turn left onto R201 for 22km. Turn right onto L1664 for 1km, then turn left. Continue for 3km, then turn sharp left. After 1km, turn right, from where another 1km will bring you to the picnic area just before the bridge.

PICNIC AREA • LAKE SWIM • EASY ACCESS

GRID REF: N 24498 99668
GOOGLE MAPS REF:
53.94591, -7.62762

⟨202⟩ ROSSES POINT AND DRUMCLIFF

COUNTY SLIGO

Sligo town is steeped in history and mythology, a vibrant place of art, music and poetry. Its lakes, beaches, mountains and ancient sites have inspired generations of stories and adventure.

North west from Sligo town is the popular Rosses Point, a bustling holiday town with a thriving yacht club. Beside the club, a juxtaposition of walls and steps forms an open-sea pool where families of all ages enjoy the summer weather; children run along the low walls while others swim or dive in the pool.

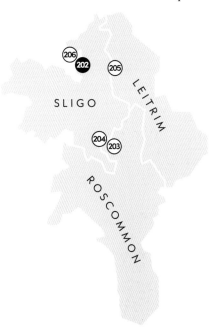

Close by, the Metal Man stands 3.6m tall on a pillar on top of Perch Rock, with the strong current sweeping below. He has pointed to the safe deep channel between Rosses Point and Coney Island since 1821. It is said that occasionally he walks back to shore for a drink, but he must have been in a hurry to return to his post: check out his mis-buttoned tunic.

If you prefer a longer swim, enter the water here and strike out to the right, across the 1.5km bay, which spans two sandy beaches. **To the left and around the point towards the yacht club, the currents are very strong and not safe for swimming**.

The pool and the first beach can be busy on summer days but walk a little farther along the shore to the second beach, which is far less crowded. For a very secluded swim, walk the full length of this second beach alongside the golf course and over the north headland to a third, almost deserted beach, which sits on the spit of land that juts north from Rosses Point across Drumcliff Bay. Several tracks lead through the dunes down to the estuary where in the shallow waters you may see daisies growing underwater beside seaweed, hermit crabs carrying their tiny shells through the grass and the sun shining through the shallow, briny water, creating a haze of gold underfoot.

On your return to the main road, take N15 to Drumcliff and visit the grave of W.B. Yeats under the shadow of Benbulben.

ABOVE AND LEFT
Rosses Point

AT A GLANCE

202 ROSSES POINT AND DRUMCLIFF

See the Metal Man at Rosses Point; dip and jump in the open-sea pool or stretch out on a long swim across the bay's two sandy beaches. Strong currents lie to the left, on the yacht club side, but to the right, towards the beaches, the bay is safe to swim. Walk across the dunes to the mouth of the estuary, wading through the shallows with daises at your feet.

BY CAR: 11 minutes from Sligo town. Take R291 north west to Rosses Point, where there is plenty of parking space. Walk past the yacht club to the point and the sea pool.

POPULAR • SEA POOLS AND BEACHES • STRONG CURRENTS • SCENIC WALK

GRID REF: G 62509 39922
GOOGLE MAPS REF:
54.30883, -8.57095

203 DOON SHORE, LOUGH KEY

A hive of activity in the summer with SUPs, kayaking and families enjoying the waters, this can be a boisterous place during the holidays. The beach area provides a safe spot for children to play in the shallows and stronger swimmers enjoy access from two pontoons.

If it's a peaceful retreat you want, choose off season. Steeped in myth and legend, Lough Key is named after Cé, one of a magical race of druids. Wounded in battle, Cé fled and made his way to this beautiful, flower-filled valley, only to die on reaching it. When his grave was dug, the lake burst out, flooding the area.

For family adventures, check out Lough Key Forest & Activity Park's trails, the Boda Borg (47 rooms of active puzzles) or explore underground tunnels to the tree-top walkway. Gardeners, stop in at The Gardens as you leave the forest.

BY CAR: 29 minutes from Sligo. Take N4 south, passing Lough Arrow. Turn left onto L1013. Continue for 38km, then turn right, signed Doon Shore. Continue for 600m to the shore.

FAMILY FRIENDLY • POPULAR • PARKING

GRID REF: G 82567 05409
GOOGLE MAPS REF:
53.99761, -8.26675

204 BALLINAFAD SLIPWAY, LOUGH ARROW

Just a few minutes from Ballinafad, this sheltered cove provides perfect access into the lough for boats, kayaks, SUPs and swimmers. Make your way out from the sheltered cove through the tall reeds to enjoy the tranquillity of the surrounding countryside. When the water is high, the C-shaped jetty lies just submerged so you can get those 'walking on water' shots! Inside this jetty is very shallow so can get thick with waterweed from late summer into autumn. Out in the deeper water, this is not an issue.

Famous as a trout-fishing lake, the lough now welcomes all types of water users. Along the roadside, this clean gravel beach gives access for boats and swimmers.

BY CAR: 25 minutes from Sligo town. Take N4 south to Ballinafad. Turn left to follow the shore road for 700m, to a deep lay-by for parking. Remember to leave the slipway clear for boats.

SCENIC LAKE SWIM • POPULAR • SWIMMING, FISHING AND KAYAKING

GRID REF: G 78745 08920
GOOGLE MAPS REF:
54.02925, -8.32518

(205) PARKE'S CASTLE, LOUGH GILL

Search for Yeats' Lake Isle of Innisfree, the uninhabited island on Lough Gill near where the poet spent his childhood summers. Parke's Castle is the point where the Lough Gill 10km swim starts, tracing the length of the lake to turn into Garvoge River and finish with a little river-flow assistance at the rowing club at Doorly Park. This is also where the *Rose of Innisfree* boat runs daily tours at midday from Easter to September so, unless you are part on the organised Lough Gill swim, make sure to avoid swimming at this time. (Correct at time of writing. Check Rose of Innisfree website for updates.) The castle is open from 17 March to 5 November.

A small public slipway beside Parke's Castle provides easy access. Keep close to shore for a totally different view of this 17th-century castle. **For longer swims, be sure to take boat cover**: a kayak is the perfect accompaniment.

By car: 14 minutes from Sligo town. Take N16 and then R286 east out of Sligo town and follow the signs for Parke's Castle.

LOUGH SWIM • BOAT TOURS • USE KAYAK COVER FOR LONGER SWIMS

GRID REF: G 78295 35107
GOOGLE MAPS REF:
54.26431, -8.33407

Raghly

(206) RAGHLY

On the narrow neck of the isthmus that is Raghly, there are two beaches. An Trá Ghearr, behind the high bank of stones, is one of the few beaches that's swimmable at low tide. At high water, the sand is completely covered and the waves race up against a barrier of stones, which is steep and difficult to walk on. However, at low water, the sand is revealed and there is only a short walk in to reach swimming depth and you remain well inside the cove formed between the mainland and Raghly isthmus. **Stormy days will provide no shelter here** so swim safe always.

A 3km loop walk takes you from here along a coastal track, past a blowhole and down onto the quiet road to Raghly Harbour, finally returning to the car park, a good way to warm up after your swim.

BY CAR: 25 minutes from Sligo town. Take N15 north to Drumcliff. After 8km, turn left onto L3305, for 2km. Turn left and continue for 6km, then turn left towards Raghly. Continue for 4km. Car parking is on the roadside.

CAUTION SHOULD BE USED • EXPOSED SWIM

GRID REF: G 57943 42670
GOOGLE MAPS REF:
54.33102, -8.64819

Spencer Harbour,
County Leitrim

TIPS FOR WINTER SWIMMING

What to expect

Cold water can take your breath; it may feel that your chest is tight and it's difficult to breathe. Focus on breathing out gently and swim at first with your head up. When you are ready to put your face in, your cheeks may burn with the cold. Sometimes we can get an 'ice-headache'; to prevent this; wear a swim cap (or two!). Even a woolly hat, if you swim head up, will help. After some time in the water, your hands will become very cold, they will stop feeling the water properly and you may even find that your little finger stretches out to the side and no amount of mental force will entice it back into line. Remember, you'll want to be able to use your hands to dress after, so don't stay in too long!

Take your time getting in

Allow your breathing to settle. In the cold we often breathe more heavily so don't let this panic you. You won't be able to swim the distances you can in summer, but you can still enjoy shorter excursions.

Join others

There are hundreds of swim groups around the country. Don't be afraid to walk up to anyone who looks like they're about to swim; they are almost always happy to share tips about the area. Charity dips are another great option for moral support and camaraderie.

Ear plugs

It's important to protect our ears. Repeated cold water and wind in the ear can cause 'swimmer's ear', a painful condition and potentially damaging to your long-term hearing. Keep ears dry, wear a cap and pull on a hat when you're out of the water too.

RIGHT Fenit Beach, County Kerry

TIPS FOR NIGHT SWIMMING

Swimming by moonlight is a particularly magical experience: to swim into the silvery thread of water lit up by a full moon with the unknown darkness surrounding that faint glimmer of light is a surreal adventure. Highlight this beautiful experience with a small group of like-minded friends.

To get the full benefit, it needs a little advance preparation; things look very different in the dark so choose a site you are familiar with and a swim buddy you are confident in.

Decide the boundaries of your swimming area and bring a lantern, torch or bright glow sticks to mark your entry and exit point, and ensure you stay within the visual limits of this light.

If this is a silent dip under a full moon, there is no need for swimmers to wear glow sticks on their person. If, however, this is a training swim or even a large group of swimmers, it is very good practice to use these or waterproof swimmers' lights. Tuck the light or glow stick under the goggle strap at the back. Some swimmers tie a length of string and tow it from their waist. The choice is yours! Glow sticks are readily available in outdoor and fishing stores.

If you are going for a long night swim with boat and kayak cover, remind the boat crew that if a torch is shone directly on the swimmer, the blinding light is all they will see. Again, glow sticks taped to the bow and stern of the boat will help the swimmer travel in the right direction; additional glow sticks near the paddle blades allow the swimmer to gauge their distance in order not to get clipped.

Finally, at nighttime the air temperature is considerably lower than during the day so bring extra warm clothing, hot drinks and even have a barbecue, if it is permitted. Save any alcohol for the after-swim celebrations.

Under no circumstances should you swim after taking any alcohol.

RIGHT Moonlight swim, Helen's Bay

TIPS FOR FRONT CRAWL

A few lessons will do wonders for your confidence and skills, but here are some general tips.

Breathe out underwater and practise breathing bilaterally. Breathing to both sides builds a more balanced stroke and means you can breathe away from wind and waves if necessary.

Use your legs

Although they don't provide a lot of propulsion in front crawl, kicking will help to lift the legs higher in the water, giving you a more horizontal body position. The result is less drag and swimming becomes easier. Lean into the water, trying to feel your heels at the surface. If the legs are low and waves are coming from behind, they can push the legs farther down; by developing a strong kick you can get the feet and legs up to the surface to take advantage of the wave and surf along instead!

Aim for a long stroke

Stretch your arm forward before starting to pull and finish the stroke near the hip. Try to travel as far as you can with each stroke rather than moving the arms as quickly as you can.

Spot where you are going

Lifting your eyes to look forward regularly during your swim will keep you on course. In the sea, rivers and lakes, there are no black lines to follow. 'Crocodile eyes' allow you to spot and then drop your head back into the water without breaking the rhythm of your

stroke. Practise this technique in the pool. In open water, choose an object easy to see, for example a church spire.

Develop a high elbow recovery

Keeping the arm high on the recovery (the over-the-water phase of the stroke) helps ensure your hands will clear the water in choppy conditions.

Swimming head up front crawl, water-polo style, is a useful drill to increase kick power, the high elbow technique and looking forward: a three-in-one drill!

Practise your skills in the pool and then develop them in the open water.

Many swimmers prefer swimming breaststroke or side stroke; these are the easiest strokes to use if you want to have a conversation, take photos or drink in the scenery.

Front crawl

Waves and bodysurfing

Bodysurfing can be great fun and utterly exhausting: the energy used to sprint in front of the drawing wave and then the exhilarating rush of boiling white water around your shoulders as you ride the breaking crest towards the beach. Be prepared to be tossed and tumbled as you try to regain your feet before the next wave rushes to meet the shore.

Getting into the sea through waves

Present as little surface area to the breaker as possible and try to avoid swimming through the white water by diving through the breaking wave.

Getting out of the sea through waves

Catch the top of the wave and bodysurf in, keep your arms in front of you and be careful of strong waves on steeply shelving beaches where the strong downward force can 'dump' the swimmer. Don't bodysurf in these conditions.

TRAINING FOR LONGER SWIMS

If you're planning to do a longer swim, train smart: setting up a training plan that will build you to your goal is imperative. Once you have decided on your challenge, analyse where you are right now. To prepare for this new challenge you will need to consider skills, endurance, speed, recovery, mental preparation and nutrition. Build all of these into your training plan.

Skills

We can all improve on our swim technique; if Olympians still have coaches to help them shave off those final hundredths of a second, the rest of us can certainly benefit from technique work. If you don't feel you need or want a coach, still do not neglect technique during your sessions. Adding drills to improve body position, balance and rotation in front crawl can make a huge difference to the ease with which you swim. Swim easier – swim farther!

Endurance

Increasing our load over time will help build our strength and swim fitness. You may need to up your time in the water and the number of sessions each week, but this will depend on your current training and your goal. Endurance does not have to be all continuous long slogs. Intervals with short rest can be as beneficial, and often more, in building long-distance endurance and maintaining a steady pace.

Speed

You may not be planning a sprint but even distance swimmers will need to turn the power on from time to time. If it's a long race, you need to be able to burst into speed for various tactics: at the start to get a good race position, overtaking another swimmer during the race, or a sprint finish. Marathon swimmers (anything over 10km) also train their speed, first, to maintain a reasonable pace and second, for sea swimmers in particular, to be able to power through when conditions require it. For example, during my channel swim I was asked at hour 7 to 'give us a good strong half hour, the tide is turning.' Having worked at speed and endurance, I knew what pace was 'strong' for me and how long I could maintain such pace.

Recovery

It is vital that we factor recovery into our training. It's as we rest that our bodies repair and adapt, becoming stronger. Work out a plan that will give you a recovery day(s) each week and on a cycle through the training year. For marathons, I find it useful to build for four to six weeks and then take an easy recovery week. I take my easy week very easy indeed, dropping my training load to almost pre-programme levels and enjoying the extra time it gives me. This allows my body to recover and

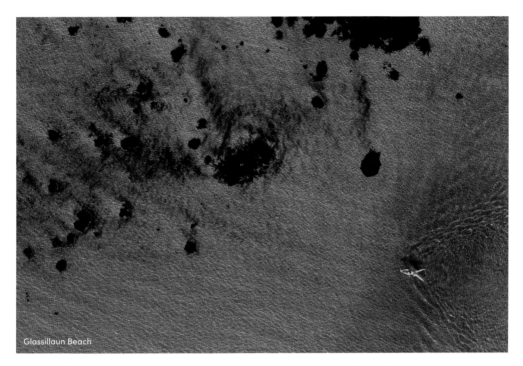
Glassillaun Beach

keep injury free, and by the end of the week I am 'raring to go'. It saves me from getting jaded and overwhelmed – see also Mental Preparation. Also, factor in your taper – reducing your exercise levels in the days before your swim event. If you haven't done the work by now, cramming isn't going to cut it and will probably result in injury.

Mental preparation

As above, tailoring in easy or recovery weeks helps me to maintain my focus. In the middle of a hard or ridiculously long swim, I can draw on the knowledge that my reward is that easy week coming up. Prepare yourself for the widest range of conditions possible; swimming for hours in the dark can be an incredibly lonely and scary place. Wind and waves can rise up unexpectedly, forcing you to dig deep and push through. For channel swimmers the possibility of not completing is very high, so prepare for that disappointment but know that you did all you could. If the conditions stop you, so be it.

Nutrition

Find what works for you. There is a multitude of energy formulas, gels and supplements available. It's highly individual deciding what works for you, so plan and practise to find your fit. The first step is a healthy balanced diet as you need to fuel your body. For marathons, you also need to fuel during the swim (so the 'no swimming for two hours after eating' rule is out!). Small and regular feeds are key; give yourself some options for variety and try them out. If something makes you feel ill, try something else. Remember that the first swimmers to complete the channel had beef tea and chicken broth! We have so much more choice now. Seasickness is a possibility so plan foods you can stomach easily. Make sure you practise your feeds in training and don't change on the day.

Six months to a 15km swim

Building up to a long-distance swim requires a simple formula, tried and tested by many marathon swimmers: build for so many weeks up to a long swim and then take a recovery week.

For 10km and above, you do not need to have completed the full distance before your event; completing a swim of 75 per cent is adequate. This prevents a swimmer overtraining and injuring themselves. Build the long swims incrementally through your training year, for example:

3 SWIMS PER WEEK

1st month: long swim – 5km

2nd month: long swim – 7km

3rd month: long swim – 9km

4th month: long swim – 11km

5th month: long swim – 13km

6th month: two-week taper to event

Each week put in a speed session and an endurance session. The third session can be whichever you prefer. Skills should form part of each session, be it warm up, cool down or within the main set. Doing one long swim each month allows you to test your progress. Recovery after this long swim can aid in injury prevention and motivation.

Gather information from others, then formulate your plan to suit your goals, your time commitment and your preferences. Remember, as we age, we may need more recovery time; avoiding injury is key. As you progress through your training, you will feel yourself getting stronger and your confidence growing.

RIGHT It is a lovely thing to swim in the rain, the surface of the water softened, broken by the raindrops ... seeing the tiny splashes each time you turn and breathe ... feeling the cool rain on your arms as you take each stroke.

JELLYFISH

Baby Lion's Mane jellyfish

Wildlife is something we need to consider as we enter the natural environment. Much of it we can harm and some can harm us. The swimmer's most dreaded animal is the jellyfish. Some get the shivers just thinking of it and some only swim in the winter when jellyfish are less prevalent. But is our fear justified? In Ireland's waters we commonly see the following native jellyfish species.

COMMON JELLYFISH, also known as moon jellyfish can give a very mild sting (less painful than a nettle!). Transparent with four purple gonad rings in the bell and very small tentacles around the edge, they are generally found April to September and can bloom in large numbers. Small but can grow up to 40cm in diameter.

COMPASS JELLYFISH

can sting; most will find this uncomfortable but not unbearable. They can be white to yellow in colour with a distinctive brown V pattern around the bell. Long tentacles and frilly mouth arms. Found July to September and can grow to 50cm in diameter.

BARREL JELLYFISH don't sting but advice tells us they cause a reaction with prolonged exposure – I can't see too many of us cuddling a jelly, though! White with a large dome and eight thick mouth-arms. They are solid and can reach 1m in diameter. Found July to September.

BLUE JELLYFISH are less common but give a strong sting. Translucent with a blue/purple ring and masses of tentacles, they grow to 30cm in diameter. Found April to July.

LION'S MANE JELLYFISH
can give a severe sting. Ranging
from yellow to deep red, the oral
arms do indeed look like the thick
mane of a lion! Numerous long fine
tentacles can trail for many metres.
They can grow extremely large, up
to 2m in diameter. Found mostly in
the cooler waters and prevalent in
the North Channel.

PELAGIA JELLYFISH are small
and less common and can sting.
10cm, like a closed fist, they have
lumps over the bell and eight
tentacles. Found autumn and winter.

VELELLA VELELLA or
by-the-wind sailor can give a mild
sting. They are not true jellyfish.
Small blue disc up to 8cm with a
transparent sail that catches the
wind. Sometimes washed on shore
in huge numbers. Found year round.

SEA GOOSEBERRY is not
a jellyfish and doesn't sting. Up
to 20cm long and shaped like a
gooseberry, it is transparent with 8
comb rows that can catch the light
with an iridescence.

PORTUGUESE MAN O'WAR
comes with a warning of severe
stings! Not a true jellyfish, it has a
large float up to 30cm long and
10cm wide. Colour can be silver
blue to purple and the tentacles
can be many metres long. Rare in
Irish waters.

Velella Velella

WHAT TO DO IF STUNG:
- Leave the water
- Seek advice from lifeguards if
  you are on a lifeguarded beach
- Rinse the area with sea water or
  try to remove tentacles – don't
  rub as that only causes more
  venom to be released
- Mild stings can be treated with
  paracetamol/ibuprofen, itching
  with antihistamine
- Apply a cold pack
- Portuguese man o'war stings:
  treat with hot water

DON'T
- Rub the area
- Rinse with fresh water
- Use vinegar, alcohol or pee!
- Use a tight bandage

Seek medical assistance if there
are any symptoms of breathing
difficulty, chest tightness, swelling
of mouth, lips or tongue.

Download the Irish jellyfish ID
PDF or join in the Big Jellyfish Hunt
online with Explore Your Shore.ie

INDEX

We would like to thank all the swimmers we have met along the way, sharing swims, stories and their favourite spots. Thank you to the team at Gill for their patience and professionalism in editing and design. We hope you enjoy this book and are inspired to explore our beautiful island.

Happy swim-sploring!

Maureen and Paul

RIGHT Devenish Island, County Fermanagh